EXCELLENCE, EQUITY, AND EFFICIENCY

How Principals and Policymakers Can Survive the Triangle of Tension

Robert T. Hess

ScarecrowEducation
Lanham, Maryland • Toronto • Oxford
2005

Published in the United States of America
by ScarecrowEducation
An imprint of The Rowman & Littlefield Publishing Group, Inc.
4501 Forbes Boulevard, Suite 200, Lanham, Maryland 20706
www.scarecroweducation.com

PO Box 317
Oxford
OX2 9RU, UK

British Library Cataloguing in Publication Information Available

Library of Congress Cataloging-in-Publication Data
Hess, Robert T. (Robert Thomas), 1962–
   Excellence, equity, and efficiency : how principals and policymakers
can survive the triangle of tension / Robert T. Hess.
      p. cm.
   Includes bibliographical references and index.
   ISBN 1-57886-202-7 (pbk. : alk. paper)
   1. School principals—United States. 2. School improvement programs—
United States. 3. Politics and education—United States. I. Title.
LB2831.92.H45 2005
371.2'012—dc22

                                                       2004020655

∞™ The paper used in this publication meets the minimum requirements of
American National Standard for Information Sciences—Permanence of Paper
for Printed Library Materials, ANSI/NISO Z39.48-1992.
Manufactured in the United States of America.

CONTENTS

INTRODUCTION

School principals in America are facing immense pressure. The pressure comes from the public, is funneled by policymakers, and is fueled by accountability to excellence, equity, and efficiency. This situation is not going to change any time soon. A Wallace Foundation survey of over 2,000 principals and superintendents revealed that more than 80 percent of them believe the demand for standards, testing, and accountability is here to stay (Johnson 2004). The same survey confirmed educators' concerns about implementing special education law and the effect of shrinking resources:

> Across the United States, public school superintendents and principals are frustrated by problems that get in the way of improving schools. Money, not surprisingly, is the most pressing issue, and most administrators report that budget problems have gotten worse in recent years. (Johnson 2004, 24)

The purpose of this book is to understand how principals manage the tension associated with change driven by the need to achieve excellence, equity, and efficiency and to discover strategies principals can pursue to effectively balance and survive these demands. Principals and school leaders across the country are scrambling to discover ways to unleash the next breakthrough in public education—success for all with dwindling resources. This book, written by a practitioner in the field, is my attempt to help that effort.

Over the past four decades, much has been written about excellence, equity, and efficiency, but the discussion here centers on how these demands can be balanced and even used to generate school improvement. This book contains a rich research base that traces the movements of excellence, equity, and efficiency in America, along with a history of accountability. However, the foundation of this project is conversations with principals. Data gleaned from these interviews are categorized as *critical incidents*—actual events and situations—principals have faced while attempting to manage the demands of excellence, equity, and efficiency.

Principals were interviewed from large urban high schools and middle schools, large suburban high schools and middle schools, medium and small rural high schools, and K–8 buildings. These schools have a wide range of poverty, affluence, and diversity. Twenty percent of the principals interviewed were members of minority groups, and 30 percent were women. The schools represent a wide geographical region of the Northwest. Altogether, I recorded 339 critical incidents in my conversations with these principals.

In my interviews I focused mostly on principals of secondary schools because the sheer size of these schools and the fact that students share teachers creates additional layers of complexity. I assumed that this complexity would add to the tension I was looking for in the schools. In addition, the literature of educational reform and school improvement reveals that high schools and middle schools are not showing the gains we are beginning to see in elementary schools. Reformer Michael Fullan is so bold as to say, "Whatever success has occurred has been at the elementary level. There are no examples of high school reform in numbers, only the odd exceptional success" (2003, 41). Hopefully the ideas and concepts presented in this book can contribute to the efforts of those working to improve secondary school environments.

Even though the focus of my conversations was secondary principals, elementary school principals, policymakers, and teacher/administrator preparation programs will find both the content and applications valuable. All of us must deal with demands for excellence, equity, and efficiency. We are all struggling with the *triangle of tension*.

Chapter 1 introduces the triangle of tension and covers several critical incidents principals have faced in their attempt to balance these important values. I discuss how the interaction of these values creates a pressure-filled environment for today's public school principal.

Chapters 2, 3, and 4 look at the historical and current movements of excellence, equity, and efficiency. Included in these chapters are critical incidents and definitions from principals about what these values mean to them, as well as how they manage them in their schools.

Chapter 5 describes the history of accountability and discusses innovations and successes principals have experienced in balancing accountability demands for excellence, equity, and efficiency. The creative power for leadership and problem solving in the midst of shrinking budgets is truly astounding.

Chapter 6 represents a shift in the book as I move from research-based theory to a framework for surviving the triangle of tension. The Quality School Improvement (QSI) framework is a guide, a proposed solution for understanding and successfully processing the demands for excellence, equity, and efficiency in the school setting.

Chapter 7 is a depiction of the district in which I am a principal. In Lebanon, Oregon, we are attempting to manage the triangle of tension through a concept called *priority leadership*. The chapter describes Lebanon Community School District's attempt to pursue a continuous progress model of instruction by systematically rejecting both social promotion and retention in an effort to see that all children progress through our schools at their own appropriate rate and level of learning.

Chapter 8 is my story at Pioneer School, where I am the principal of a K–8 school of 500 students. In this chapter I describe how the application of the QSI framework resulted in breakthrough achievement—as demonstrated by 90 percent of all our students achieving state benchmarks in reading and math.

Chapters 9 and 10 are recommendations and strategies for principals and policymakers to help them survive and successfully overcome the triangle of tension.

At the end of each chapter I have included questions that can be used to review important concepts presented, generate discussion, or stimulate thought for staff development and classroom exercises. I hope they are helpful.

I am a public school principal, and I love my job. Even though it is stressful most of the time, there isn't any other profession I would rather pursue, because the work I do directly affects the lives of the most important resource in the nation—our children. For many of the children attending our public schools, education *is* their only hope for a better tomorrow. It is for their benefit that the educators of this country daily find the strength to face the triangle of tension and learn how to overcome its demands. The struggle is worth the effort.

The concepts presented in this book were developed over a five-year period of great effort, learning, and continual growth. There have been countless contributors—too many to name: my outstanding teaching staff, parents, students, fellow principals who sat down with me to share their hearts, supervisors, outstanding educators, professors at the University of Oregon, the fine people at ScarecrowEducation, and my own family and friends. They all have had a part to play, and for their help I am grateful.

This book is dedicated to meeting the needs of the students in our care. May we find joy in small victories and never grow weary of pursuing this endless task.

1

VALUES THAT DRIVE CHANGE: THE TRIANGLE OF TENSION

We are precariously close to the total erosion of our infrastructure. We started to approach that this year, and we are going to be on the precipitous next year . . . and the question becomes how much can you creatively maintain the equity and excellence to keep dancing the dance—but at what point is the dance floor removed from beneath you because of the lack of basic provisions? At what point do you go to an efficiency factory model with 45 kids in a classroom and say, good luck. Unfortunately, I think that is where we are headed.
—*large suburban high school*

Education is shaped by the values of the culture and society to which it belongs. Public education has undergone a series of changes during the last four decades, and most of these changes have been driven by public policy. In addition to the increased level of accountability due to the excellence movement, school districts have been forced to become more efficient with resources. These changes are made more complex and difficult to administer by the requirements of extensive equity legislation.

Viewed systemically, the root cause of new public policy stems from the values of excellence, equity, and efficiency. Policy demands generate tension for schools and the people who manage them. However, policymakers, researchers, and other stakeholders maintain it is precisely this tension that generates school improvement. Peter Senge's work (1990) supports the notion of using creative tension to generate improvement, as did one of the principals I interviewed:

> I think that tension needs to be there. I have created that tension with my staff. It is intentional, and I am delivering that because I think they really need to get on the growth curve.—*large suburban high school*

TENSION GENERATORS: EXCELLENCE, EQUITY, AND EFFICIENCY

The values of excellence, equity, and efficiency are the chief drivers of change on the educational landscape of America. For this reason, these values can be called *tension generators* because they drive policy, generate tension, and ultimately create change for principals who are chiefly responsible for implementing reform at the school level. It is less clear, however, how these values are often in conflict with each other. The inherent tension between them makes the effective management of these values even more difficult for today's school leader, especially when it comes to real people, real jobs, and kids who really need the services. Principals constantly struggle with dilemmas that arise from this tension:

> I could be working in my office—working on the budget like I have been over the last two weeks, and the numbers, it's depressing. Already today I have had three people in my office, and I've had to tell them, you know it looks like after this year we are not going to be able to use you next year. I mean those are tough conversations.—*medium-sized rural high school*

The Triangle of Tension

A triangle can be used to depict the relationship and tension between the competing values of excellence, efficiency, and equity. In this framework, excellence is at the apex because the demand for achievement occurs most frequently. Often stated in terms of accountability, the current climate in education is one of results. Figure 1.1 is an illustration of the triangle of tension.

Figure 1.1.   **The triangle of tension.**

Although the demand for excellence is the strongest driver of change in education today, leaders must walk a tightrope—and often engage in a tug-of-war—between equity and efficiency to achieve it. The simultaneous interaction of equity, efficiency, and excellence can create a climate of chaos for today's school leader. A principal is answerable to a school board looking for results, a superintendent looking to trim the budget, and the federal government for complex equity legislation. School leaders are looking for strategies to manage and lead people to accomplish the complex task of achieving excellence while maintaining the equilibrium between equity and efficiency. As principals attest, the task is not easy:

> Next year we are operating with a scarcity model. And so I am going to have to question what are the absolute essentials I have to deliver for my kids. What is mandated? And the second thing—this sounds really

frightening—but I may get to a point where I say seniors can only enroll for six classes. Juniors for 7, sophomores and freshman, 8. We are truly moving toward scarcity times, so if you are running a depression model high school, what does that look like?—*large suburban high school*

Tomlinson (1994) has recognized a connection among efficiency, equity, and excellence. She maintains that efficiency comes into conflict with the 200-plus-year struggle to meet the competing democratic ideals of excellence and equity. Although we pay to homage to excellence with the recognition that much of our greatness as a nation has stemmed from encouraging ingenious individuals to develop their abilities, we are also shaped as a nation by the refrain and belief that all people are created equal and the notion of fairness and opportunity for all. In Tomlinson's words, "It may well be that the health of our schools, as well as our democracy, is maintained by balancing the competing ideals of excellence and equity" (1994, 32).

The Tension Between Excellence and Equity

Leaders in our country have been taking up excellence or equity since the dawn of our nation, and the roots of these conflicting values are represented in the Jeffersonian and Jacksonian concepts of education that were developed from 1789 to 1877. Thomas Jefferson advocated the development of excellent schools for the best and brightest. Andrew Jackson argued for equal access and opportunity for all. Both men felt their philosophy would best serve the public interest, and both ideals have gathered their followings through the years (Zimmerman 1997).

The pendulum has been swinging from one to the other, and every few decades a new shove generates movement in the opposite direction. Just during the last half century we can see the 1950s as a rallying call for excellence in science and mathematics education as the nation competed to send a man to the moon. In the early 1960s to mid-1970s, educational excellence was set aside for an all-out concern to provide equity to whole groups of disenfranchised Americans whose needs were not being met by the system. The pendulum swung again in the 1980s and early 1990s with a march toward high standards, and financial equity was thrown into the mix in the mid-1990s (Zimmerman 1997). And now the most recent implementation of the No Child Left Behind (NCLB) Act represents a demand for both excellence (high standards) and equity (everyone is included—no child is left behind). It is no wonder this legislation is causing such tension and stress in the public school community.

It seems we cannot get away from the tension that exists between these two values. Gardner (1961) may have defined the issue for us best with his question over forty years ago, "Can we be equal and excellent too?" That question is just as relevant today. These two values are intricately linked together, and when attention is not given to both, one will be sacrificed on the altar of the other.

For example, if standards are important, it can be argued that the same standards must be applied to all. However, if we are serious about equal opportunity, different resources must be provided to different students. School interventions must occur so that no student is held back by the progress rate of others. "Excellence without equity is elitism, and equity without excellence produces mediocrity" (Zimmerman 1997, 21), and neither position is desirable. The National Joint Committee on Learning Disabilities has gone so far as to declare that the "school reform movement may adversely affect students with learning disabilities," claiming that "these students may be ignored, and their needs unacknowledged as the initiatives of the reform movement are planned and implemented" (NJCLD 1991, 280).

An illustration of the tension between excellence and equity can be seen in Singapore. Singapore recently initiated free-market policies in their education system in an attempt to emphasize school autonomy and competition among schools. Although these policies were aimed at fostering educational excellence, the unintended consequence was a hit on equity. Schools were under increasing pressure to attract students who would be assets in terms of contributing to higher rankings in the school report cards. Students who could not raise test scores were seen as liabilities and were not as welcome in the schools (Lim and Tan 1999).

In Great Britain, the conservative reforms of the 1980s were based on the idea that it was only through the discipline of the market that schools could improve. Purchasers (parents) chose which supplier (school) they would send their children to, and funding followed the children. In principle, as more parents sent their children to the best schools, those

schools would be rewarded and expansion would take place. The unintended consequence when Great Britain initiated this excellence policy
was a narrowing of a school's focus on measurable outcomes at the expense of broader, more affective outcomes. In addition, schools in socially disadvantaged communities did not have an equal opportunity to
score as well on the achievement tests as students from more affluent
communities. Although there was nothing deterministic about the link
between the socioeconomic characteristics of school populations and
school-level examination performance, the research showed a simple
fact that the more socially disadvantaged the community served by a
school, the much more likely it is that the school will appear to be underachieving (Gibson and Asthana 1998).

Evidence of that same tension can be seen in the United States. In
the state of Massachusetts, the town of Lynnfield announced that it was
time to end METCO, a program that for twenty years had brought minority children into the nearly all-white, middle-class, suburban communities. The school board told the press that the program wasn't helping the Lynnfield schools raise their standards—in other words, their
scores on the new tough state tests were dropping. In the words of Deb-
orah Meier, who documented the incident, "Sometimes equity and excellence just don't mix well. So sorry" (2000, 4).

The principals I spoke with experienced this tension as well when it
came to cutting programs while at the same time providing extra resources for special education. Often it was the unidentified at-risk students who suffered the most:

> The equity piece, I am trying to think, I would say we don't have true eq-
> uitable services in the areas for our at-risk kids because our class sizes are
> so large—we are up to 35 in our main classes, and even though I think
> students are good at doing a lot of the work, because of the behavior is-
> sues, they are not getting it. And if we were really being equitable both
> to those who want to focus and those who need the extra help, we would
> have an alternative program, and we have no alternative program. That is
> a huge struggle. I don't think in that case we are really being equitable to
> anybody.—*medium-sized rural high school*

> As long as you are pursuing excellence, there isn't any friction, but once
> they feel threatened—my job, my activities, my kids—once that becomes

a threatening situation and efficiency becomes the goal, then there is a lot of friction. Everyone becomes focused on their priorities. Why are you thinking of cutting this program? They don't care about the others . . . why this one? So it does become contentious.—*large urban high school*

I don't know if it addresses it, but I have seen a huge shift in resources, and there is a definite pendulum swing toward funding for IDEA, and other mandated programs while the rest of our school structure is dying on the vine. District wide, we have seen the ratio of certified staff drop from 75 percent to 62 percent of the budget in the last five years. The ratio of classified assistants has gone up from 25 percent to 35 percent, and it is almost all in the special education assistant category. There is an equity mandated provision for special education students that at times really flies in the face of what is happening with the rest of the K–12 program, and I think that presents a huge dilemma for us, and I don't have an answer for that.—*large suburban high school*

I know that we as a school attempt to pump more resources into children with high needs, and that has resulted in a fair amount of success with those children, but I also know it ends up being at the expense of the other children. For example, in our 6th grade block program we have 2 periods of literature and one of social studies, but for those children we have 2 periods of reading because their skills are so low. But those teachers will throw a fit if you put more than 20 of them in one class, because to those teachers, 20 of them is like 35 of the other. So as natural result of keeping those classes small, the others become unnaturally large.—*large suburban middle school*

The Tension Between Efficiency and Equity

To illustrate how the values of efficiency and equity interact, consider the notion of introducing elements of the free market into education for the sake of efficiency. In a market-driven economic system, schools must meet the demands of the consumer or go out of business. The product and quality must change with the changing times or become obsolete (Clegg 2000). Proponents of this system argue that if education is permitted to operate with minimal government regulation, then it will become more efficient—costs will remain low while productivity improves (Okun 1975). School-choice advocates often rely on economic or efficiency concepts to support the need for school choice. In the No Child Left Behind Act, the first sanction after the two-year warning period includes school choice as an option when a school is determined to be not making adequate yearly progress (AYP). Under that sanction, parents can choose to send their children to another school in the district that is making AYP, at the school district's expense.

At present in the public system, consumers (parents and taxpayers) do not directly purchase their children's education, and they do not have autonomy in determining the nature of the school system. Local boards operate within a framework of local, state, and federal policies (Carlson 1996). However, the introduction of economic theories and marketplace strategies into the domain of public education is problematic at best because of the trade-offs with excellence and equity (Boyd and Kerchner 1988).

One side effect of operating education as a market is a trade-off with equity. Some people will achieve more than others because they will have better opportunities, and inequity will result. It doesn't take much imagination to think how the educational needs of the handicapped, for instance, would go unmet without legislation to protect their rights. Advocates of efficiency argue that such inequalities are necessary to promote the efficiency of the economic system (Friedman 1962). Those who believe education should be market-driven are leaders in the movement to adopt school-choice policies such as open enrollment, charter schools, and voucher plans (Cookson 1994). The growth of per pupil spending throughout the 1960s, 1970s, and 1980s can be traced to increased funding services for poor, disabled, and other special needs students (Lankford and Wyckoff 1995)—a direct trade-off between equity and efficiency.

Another example of how efficiency affects equity was the reauthorization of Title I in 1995. The 1995 reauthorization paved the way for schools to use Title I funds for schoolwide programs (Brown-Hedrick 2002–2003). After 1995 many districts across the country turned to their Title I dollars to support broader reform efforts rather than targeting individual students with high needs. Before 1995, all Title I money was targeted to be spent on students who qualified through identification. The 1995 legislation gave districts a choice to use the money differently with fewer restrictions, and the 2002 reauthorization of Title I (No Child Left Behind) added increased accountability (Dickson 2002) via levels of sanctions for every year a school does not make AYP.

Other researchers (Wells and Crain 1992) have critiqued the economic choice theory as a means of efficiency because it assumes that families will act rationally in a goal-oriented fashion to find the best schools when given tuition vouchers. Research on school choice suggests that parents and children consider availability of transportation as the major factor in determining their choice of schools, and that poor and minority families place a greater emphasis on the comfort and familiarity of their neighborhood school even though they may believe distant suburban schools are better (Carlson 1996).

The principals I interviewed experienced the tension between equity and efficiency frequently. The tension surfaced when it came to budgets, alternative education, programming, and implementing special education policies. Many felt that state and federal equity policies provided additional resources that could have been used more efficiently in other areas of the school program:

> I just put my budget together, and here we are cutting programs, cutting teachers, cutting athletics, and maybe even cutting an administrator, and yet I am trying to find ways to spend ESL dollars. Because we have 38.5 ESL students and that translates into 142,000 of ESL money. So, we have to spend it on ESL things. We have a teacher, that's 69,000, we have an aide, so now I'm creating things—sub money so the teacher can go look at other programs. To me, that is just lubricious having to try and find ways to spend money when everyone else is just dying.—*medium-sized rural high school*

> I think the rights have tipped too far toward parents in the issue of special education. Now most parents won't abuse that, but when you have one that does, and we certainly had one that did last year, it consumed everybody's time, and I mean everybody's. I think that legislation ought to be changed.—*large suburban high school*

> As our funding goes down, that is a piece of quality that will be lost. Because I do think if you are going to be equitable to all of the kids, you need many programs.—*medium-sized rural high school*

Budget cuts. Alternative education (programs that meet the needs of individuals) are being shifted to the regular classroom. The reduction in staffing provides less outside of the classroom opportunities which results in not being able to meet a variety of student needs.—*large urban high school*

And so, at what point does all of that get in the way? If they really gut our instructional assistant budget, we will have fewer assistants in the classrooms with the children who have the highest needs.—*large suburban middle school*

Some of the lower kids are missing out on opportunities, like not going on the trip today. That is the sad part. How do we keep things equitable with dwindling resources? I haven't figured that out yet.—*small rural high school*

Yes—our district attempts to help schools with a lower SES by giving them FTE from the schools with a higher SES. As a result, we have 1.5 less FTE here and we can't do what we need to do to maintain quality due to this equity policy.—*large urban high school*

Do we need the funding? Yes, especially in the area of bilingual education. I have a vast number of students who are bilingual in the building and if we have to have a reduction in force, the last teachers hired are the first to go instead of looking at what is needed to maintain my curriculum. They don't look at that. They look at tenure, so it is going to be very, very difficult.—*large urban middle school*

I would say that piece is tough. I have one automotive class with 8 or 9 kids in it, and it is absolutely ideal for those kids and they are doing the work and everything and they have their space, but I am not going to have that program next year. There is no way I can keep an 8 student class. That is a course they need and love, but the efficiency money-wise is just not going to hold it.—*medium-sized rural high school*

The question becomes, how do you keep up the morale of staff when you keep having to reduce resources and they keep having to do more and more with less and less. The teaching workload continues to rise with each cutback and the ratio of students to staff in alternative education is going up as well—it is harder and harder to meet those individual needs.—*large urban high school*

If you are looking in the special education department, the regulations are really stressful. You must dot your I's and cross your T's. I think there is way more paperwork than necessary, and it has become now that the paperwork is more for protection against a lawsuit than a benefit to the student . . . that is what it is about.—*medium-sized rural high school*

Equalization hurt our district. The local patrons here have been really supportive of education and we've been lucky to pass pretty much anything. But equalization has taken money out of district and sent it to the capital.—*large suburban high school*

On top of that, you have the equity with seniority. We are going to have a little shuffling of the deck. People are going to come in and not know our system and that is going to cause some loss of efficiencies there because they won't know the kids, the system, and what is going on. So being equitable in terms of financing and seniority is going to cause some loss of excellence and efficiency.—*small rural K–8*

The Tension Between Efficiency and Excellence

Efficiency can also be in conflict with excellence. Efficiency is the driving force in education resulting in curricula, instruction, pacing, and assessment shaped to meet the needs of the majority of the students, and as long as efficiency encourages drafting one curriculum per grade in a subject, developing one lesson plan for a class, teaching that lesson in one way, and defining success in one way, the apex of excellence cannot be achieved (Tomlinson 1994). The learning needs of the outliers—both above and below the mean—are consistently sacrificed to meet the demands of efficiency.

No matter how one defines an excellent educational system, the pursuit of efficiency is bound to undercut quality because education is expensive. Pursuing and achieving high standards requires up-to-date materials, well-trained teachers who are continuously learning, and relatively small classes (Fowler 2000). All of this costs money, and when money is spent, efficiency goes down.

The Nation Joint Council of Learning Disabilities (1991) understands that school reform (pursuit of excellence) and school finances are inextricably linked. The NJCLD argues that national reform movements must be coupled with careful evaluation of educational funding that provides equitable education of students with disabilities.

The principals I interviewed experienced a constant struggle between pursuing excellence and having enough resources to plan budgets, meet all of the student needs, put forth energy to develop programs to their potential, and make transportation work efficiently:

> We were satisfactory last year and strong the year before (state report card ratings), but math holds us up. We are doing all right in the other areas, but our math scores are not what we like. And there is a thing with excellence. Our teachers went through a whole assessment with the math program and determined what textbooks would best meet their needs, and now when it comes time to buy them, we don't have any money, so when you talk about excellence and efficiency, they are going to crash big time on that one.—*large suburban middle school*

> It's been a distracting year because I am wondering if I am going to have my supply budget cut or if I am going to hear from the budget manager that I am going to lose staff next year. You have to go to meeting after meeting, you have parents that are upset, and kids too—high school kids are upset. There is a lot of energy and time put into that and not being able to plan more than a month ahead with your budget is very distracting. So, it has been distracting and it has taken up time and energy on everybody's behalf.—*large suburban high school*

> For example, last year was our science adoption, and we only had money to purchase life science books; we couldn't get chemistry or physics. This year is math, so I went to the math department and said you have a choice. You can get $39,000 in textbooks or cut one-half an FTE in math. They choose to cut the FTE. We are at the point where we don't have usable textbooks in math. We are at the point where we have to make choices like that.—*medium-sized rural high school*

> Except for our reading program, I can't say we have maximized the potential of volunteers. I know there is an incredible amount of energy out there, but recruiting and managing those volunteers is a job in itself.— *large suburban high school*

> We found out that they eliminated the SIF [school improvement funds]— it was part of the free fall this last year—so entering into last fall, we had

to eliminate the program, but we didn't care. We totally believed in the program, so we are still buying two periods of reading, and we are taking it out of language arts, as a result we are letting our class sizes go way up in LA in order to provide the program.—*large suburban high school*

We have a SMART board, one of them, and the Internet, but if someone finds a new technology, we can't even get a prototype. We can't update the software. They say as long as you have a piece of slate you can teach, but that's not today's world. We want a 21st-century model and have 20th-century schools. It doesn't work.—*small rural high school*

Busing is another example of how we do not pursue best practice due to an effort to be efficient. Research tells us that older students will do better in school when they start later in the day. They need more sleep. There will be less absences and tardiness if school starts later, but the bus schedule dictates when the start time is. So since the elementary schools start a certain time, high schools start when those bus runs pick up the kids—not at the time that would be good for their learning.—*large urban high school*

How the Triangle of Tension Functions

The pursuit of excellence is connected with issues of equity and efficiency in several ways. The current education reform movement around the nation calls for higher standards for *all* students. Most states include statements to this effect in their standards documents. Although it is just a rallying cry in many places, some states have begun to take steps to hold their schools and districts accountable for the performance of all students on these new goals (Firestone et al. 1997), and new federal laws are forcing even the most reluctant to follow suit. The No Child Left Behind Act, enacted in 2002, is the most extensive legislation to date requiring states to meet certain AYP goals not only on a whole-school basis but also among subgroups of students, including minorities, the poor, and special education students. Schools that don't meet the AYP progress standards are faced with a variety of sanctions, which can include losing control of the school. Principals are frustrated with the lack of clarity about the new requirements and other state-mandated accountability requirements:

So to bring this in [NCLB] and say to people, "you are now being judged on adequate yearly progress beginning last year (but you didn't know

where you were when you did all that testing), and they are going to give
you a number in March about your AYP (which you don't really understand, because no one does) and it is going to be different from your
school report card," which is just a big joke to most people.—*large suburban middle school*

So I am telling my people now, we are not buying into this anymore. We
are going to make our own report card and we are going to report to our
community and build on their trust . . . and that is what I am going to
share with my folks. I got on my soapbox last Monday night with the
school board and our district leaders and told them that they need to understand that this is a bogus system [the state report card], and they are
completely supportive.—*large suburban high school*

Even though education is governed by state legislation, the federal
government can withhold money through Title I funding if states re-
fuse to comply with the guidelines of No Child Left Behind (Dickson
2002). In today's cash-strapped climate, schools simply cannot afford
to say no to No Child Left Behind, even though at least one reformer
has advocated that states deny the funding to send a message to the
feds that implementing the law costs more than states will receive
(Bracey 2003). As of yet, however, no state has turned down the cash.
Efficiency pressure forces compliance and cooperation even though
many educators disdainfully disagree with the tenets of No Child Left
Behind: the increased federal accountability, mandatory high-stake
testing at every grade level, and the notion that *all children* must
achieve high standards or the schools and those who work in them will
be punished.

In the realm of efficiency, state courts have begun to link school finance equity and high standards through educational adequacy cases.
As of 1995, three state courts had defined a constitutionally adequate
and equitable public school system as one that provides students with
opportunities to attain the specific skills that are necessary to be nationally and internationally competitive (Morgan, Cohen, and Hershkoff 1995).

There is also concern that disadvantaged students do not have access
to the kinds and level of educational programs needed to help them
achieve higher standards. These students arrive at school each day with

less social capital—the support and structure needed outside of school to be successful. Equity advocates have developed opportunity-to-learn standards to address this problem (Smith, Fuhrman, and O'Day 1994). These standards define a set of conditions that schools, districts, and states must meet to ensure that all students have the opportunity to achieve high standards. Unfortunately, such opportunity standards are very expensive to implement because they require a great deal of capital to be invested in poorer districts.

Excellence can be expensive in other ways. It takes money to develop outstanding programs for talented and gifted students—money that could have been spent making education more accessible to all. On the other hand, when money is spent for programs that attempt to reach at-risk and disadvantaged students in the name of equity, it is not being spent to increase the capabilities of the average or gifted child. Hence, many argue that the value of equity drives the overall system away from excellence and toward mediocrity.

CONCLUSION

The challenge for today's principal lies in achieving a balance between the competing values of excellence, equity, and efficiency and searching for ways to resolve the inherent conflicts among them. The first step in managing the tension is to understand the history of excellence, equity, and efficiency in American education. Hearing how principals wrestle with these values in their daily work will also be helpful in building a capacity to deal with the tension. The next three chapters investigate the movements of excellence, equity, and efficiency. Conversations with principals about these values are included. Listening to their stories and struggles will help us understand and discover new ways to successfully survive the tension associated with change and school improvement driven by the pressure of excellence, equity, and efficiency.

Discussion Points

1. Describe how the values of excellence, equity, and efficiency have driven change in your school or district.

2. Would you agree or disagree with the idea that tension created from seeking to meet the demands of excellence, equity, and efficiency generates school improvement? Why or why not?
3. Describe how the triangle of tension operates in your school or district. Can you think of any specific examples?
4. What are some of the possible solutions for managing the triangle of tension you experience in your position?
5. In what ways does determining priorities help in resolving the inherent tension among these values in your school?

② THE PURSUIT OF EXCELLENCE

Excellence is a habit. I get that from Aristotle. What you do is what you become. What you do is what you are. He talked about moral excellence. Just do little habits and they become part of you. That's what excellence is. Doing little things over time become big things. Vince Lombardi, one of my heroes, said the quality of a man's life is in direct proportion to his commitment to excellence. Excellence is a personal modeling that is a part of our character. It is our reflection. It is our entire being. We stress to become excellent. I am looking to become better. Each thing I do each day makes me better. And that is how I define excellence.—*small rural high school*

HISTORICAL EXCELLENCE

What is excellence and how do we measure it? Educators, reformers, and researchers have shaped and reshaped what we call excellence, and all of these definitions are a part of excellence today. Gardner (1961) defined excellence as striving for quality in all areas of society. Gross (1989) saw excellence as the need to achieve, the success drive, and motivation to learn at high levels. Silverman (1993) maintained that excellence cannot be defined as success because our culture does not recognize the contributions of many disenfranchised groups. Roeper (1996) viewed excellence as a standard for gifted students to achieve—learning to develop as ethical and moral human beings. VanTassel-Baska (1997) defined excellence as both a process of working toward an ideal standard and the attainment of a high standard of performance in an endeavor valued by society. However, it is Thomas Jefferson's views on excellence in education that have shaped much of the system we have in place today.

Jefferson proposed the notion that colleges should be established in which superior students would be educated to contemplate great works of art, literature, and nature in preparation for leadership roles in society—the Harvard and Yale of yesterday and today. He believed that superior students from any class could rise to leadership roles based on ability, but he also held fast to the notion of a privileged class of students (Zimmerman 1997).

The majority of participants in my research defined excellence in terms of success. In every case, excellence was more than what could be quantified by test score results or attendance rates. In the words of the principals, excellence also included things that cannot be easily quantified, such as a student's connection to school, commitment to learning, involvement in the community, and the appeal of the facilities:

> Excellence is both quantitative and subjective. I would define it as a value judgment of being the best, or achieving your goal, achieving the right stuff. Individual student excellence would be determining where they are and deciding where they need to be to be a better student, person, member of society—a contributor for themselves and others and what it will take to get them there. Moving toward that optimal development where each kid is—knowing where they are and seeing what they need to get there.—*small rural K–8*

> To me excellence is pushing beyond the minimum you have to do to say that you are good and really reaching for what you can do to be great, and in terms of excellence in this middle school it is going out and seeking out ways we can make life really good for the people that are here—the students, the teachers, the staff, so that they can walk out of here saying, "we like it here."—*large suburban middle school*

Success. By that I mean it is not a set standard. It is means different things for different kids. The finish line isn't the same and neither is the starting line. It is a progression.—*medium-sized rural high school*

In the educational climate of today, excellence as a value stems from the demand for quality. Fowler (2000) and others (Heimann and Sikula 2001–2002; Brown-Hedrick 2002–2003) have traced the modern educational reform movement of excellence back to 1983 with the publication of *A Nation at Risk* (National Commission on Excellence in Education 1983). The publication was a list of recommendations from hearings the NCEE had held across the country. The NCEE concluded that education in the United States suffered from a lack of rigor and did not allow sufficient time for children to learn adequately. The commission also found that teachers were poorly prepared and underpaid, and it issued some general recommendations, including the following: increase basic requirements of English, math, science, and social studies; adopt more rigorous and measurable standards; significantly increase the time devoted to learning the basics; increase teacher preparation; and encourage citizens to get involved in the process and hold leaders accountable for results (Edwards and Wallace 1993).

In general, the report was received with criticism from the educational community, which felt it was a politically motivated attack on public schools initiated by the Reagan administration. The main premise behind the report was that achievement test scores were the primary measure of a good environment. Standing behind that belief was an attack on the very idea of *public*: Whatever was public was bad; private was good (White 1993). In essence, the commission claimed that public schools had failed, and its message resulted in a call from business and political leaders for educational reform (Gardner 1984; Helbowitsh 1990). The report took a top-down approach that focused on tightening standards and increasing accountability; it led to a "virtual tidal wave of bureaucratic mandates from state government to improve education" (Lunenburg 1992, 4). It wasn't long afterward that outcome-based education and standards (already a staple of business) were developed extensively, state by state.

Today's principals feel the pressure to show improvement in ways that can be measured, and most of those I interviewed work hard at tracking data for their constituents to prove they are being successful:

> If you and I were to look at the data, you would see that our dropout rate has been the lowest these last two years than at any other time. We went up a little this year—I am disappointed, but we've had two consecutive years below 5 percent and we are going to continue to drive that down. We have had higher numbers graduating. When I first got here, we graduated about 220 kids a year and this year we are going to graduate 290.—*large suburban high school*

> We also look at attendance and dropout rates. Our dropouts have really gone down, and our attendance rate has gone up to 92 percent. It was really in the low 80's when we started a couple of years ago. Test scores have not been as good as I want them. Frankly speaking we have some problems with math. We've had 6 teachers in the last 5 years. We are trying to get that stable. In writing we are way ahead, and in reading we are a little above average. We are working at it.—*small rural high school*

> I looked at our state assessment scores, especially math. I looked at our dropout rate. I looked at the minority dropout rate and the state report card. So that was the focus of last three years, and we have had significant impact on those areas. The short answer is you have to narrow the focus of where you extend your energies. Whereas we used to expend it over a broad range of activities, now you have focus it on what you and your community feel is important to your school. —*medium-sized rural high school*

Around the same time that *Nation at Risk* appeared, Theodore Sizer (1984) conducted a three-year study of public high schools. His research revealed that the structure of high schools in the 1980s resembled the structure of nineteenth-century high schools: isolated subjects, accumulated credits toward graduation, specific hours and days in school, students as passive receptors in the learning process, and so on. After all, in 1893 the Committee of Ten, under the leadership of a Harvard University president, had recommended a common curriculum for all secondary students that urged high schools to teach four years of English and three years of history, science, mathematics, and a foreign language—a common curriculum that high schools today across the nation are still religiously pursuing (Carlson 1996). Sizer's report, coming on the heels of *A Nation at Risk*, sent the bells of reform ringing.

DEMONSTRATIONS OF EXCELLENCE

The desire for excellence in American education is a recurring response to national crises. After the Soviets launched *Sputnik* in 1957, magazines throughout the states fired off articles critical of U.S. schools. *Life* magazine featured an essay by Sloan Wilson that declared a list of faults: The diploma had declined to meaninglessness, the rise of electives had swept out academic rigor, textbooks were watered down, and students no longer learned the basics (Braccy 1994). Not long afterward the federal government enacted the National Defense Education Act and funded development in mathematics and science education

Unlike equity, which focuses on the differences among students, school, and districts, and efficiency, which looks at operations and costs, the excellence movement seeks to increase the scope and rigor of educational programs so that students are better prepared to overcome the perceived threat (Firestone et al. 1997).

As *Sputnik* had launched an educational tidal wave of math and science curriculum, so *A Nation at Risk* in 1983 set sail standards-based education. The perceived threat in the 1980s was that Americans were not prepared to maintain the nation's competitive economic position (Firestone et al. 1997). The fear was that we couldn't produce students capable of keeping the United States on top of the standard-of-living chart. However, the 1990s demonstrated that our schools were not so much at risk after all. The United States ranked second in the world for elementary school literacy, the productivity of our workforce was near the top, and our system of advanced education was the envy of the world (Meier 2000).

When this news quietly hit the scene, the excellence movement found its new home in competitiveness, with a host of alternatives to public schools vying for students, including home schools, private schools, virtual off-site schools via the Internet, charter schools, for-profit schools, and voucher programs. Currently, only 25 percent of American households contain school-aged children, so public schools now must demonstrate their excellence simply to keep their constituents (Heimann and Sikula 2001–2002).

Principals are under tremendous pressure to demonstrate excellence, and it is clear that they believe differentiation of instruction, focused curriculum, and high expectations are key factors to achieving it:

Differentiation of instruction is the key to achieving excellence. Teachers try to do the best with what they have, but the question to keep asking is: Are we ascribing to best practice, or are we just getting by? The reform has not driven what we do here, good practice does. We pursue good practice.—*large urban high school*

When it comes to excellence, we started by asking what we were teaching. As a result, a lot of the pet projects are disappearing. We had one teacher who only taught *Lord of the Flies* for 19 or 20 years in a row. That's all he would teach for the entire semester. Well, it didn't fit the appropriateness of the curriculum for his grade level, so that has gone away. We've had a lot of good things like that occur instructionally.—*small rural high school*

Excellence is our motto. I do not accept excuses for not doing homework. I do not accept excuses for bad grades. I require students to have the opportunity to redo assignments until they reach that state of excellence. Here we work with students where they are and take them where they need to be.—*large urban middle school*

According to the principals, excellence can also be demonstrated via innovative programs and schoolwide restructuring of how students spend their time in school:

We are achieving excellence in the very strong programs that have been recognized by the state or nationally. These include our programs in recycling, community service, and we have one heck of a great garden, and we have children that feel a strong connection to the school, and I think that is one way that we are excellent. We try to do more and more with our physical plant. It's not unusual for me to get out my painting clothes and paint a wall or look at an area and create something new because I think it is something the people would like. And so I think in the matters of the heart, our school is achieving excellence and we are very open to what more we could be doing.—*large suburban middle school*

We have a couple of departments here that are absolutely outstanding. The first is our science department, which to me I would put against any school in the state. It is very hands on, and very much community oriented. Our ecology class is connected with the farm industry and a catalog company. We grow things for them. Lettuce is one thing we grow. We grow different varieties of lettuce and the students provide all of the data to the company, and the company decides which seeds they want to sell. It is a wonderful partnership. The same group is also working with a company that manufactures DNA. It is being shipped all over the world. The hospitals send them a request for certain linkage of DNA, and then the company makes it and sends it back to the hospital. Our students are involved with these projects. These programs became excellent because of their unique types of instruction.—*medium-sized rural high school*

Two years ago our scores were really poor, but we have made some site-based decisions and we have truly, truly caused our scores to soar. One of the decisions we made was to redefine our block schedule. Instead of having math every other day, our students have math every day, and our math scores have truly gone up from that, which is a demonstration that excellence can be achieved by adjusting instruction.—*large urban middle school*

CONCLUSION

Principals define excellence in terms of success or achievement. That success is not always academic or easily quantified, but it can be seen and felt. Academic excellence is influenced primarily by improved instruction. The excellence movement in education isn't going away—ever. It may change its focus and direction from time to time, but there will always be an emphasis on achievement and improvement. This isn't news to practicing principals.

Discussion Points

1. How does the pressure to achieve excellence manifest itself in your school?

2. What laws or policies are influenced by the value of excellence in your district?
3. In what ways is your school or district achieving excellence?
4. How would you measure an excellent climate or environment?
5. How would you measure academic excellence?
6. What would your school or district look like if there was no external pressure to achieve excellence?

3

THE PROMISE OF EQUITY

Equity is not treating all kids the same. Equity is creating different avenues of opportunity that are the highest predictor of success for all kids, regardless of circumstance. Each avenue may look a little be different, so it is not one size fits all. It is many, many different avenues, but it is an outcome that I will guarantee as a school leader that every kid will have an opportunity to get to that final ideal outcome.—*large urban high school*

Historically, the value of equity has been a strong driver of change on the educational landscape, and often parents, policymakers, and educators have differing perceptions of what equity means. Reviewing the historical role of equity will help us understand how we can apply it in schools today.

HISTORICAL EQUITY

In a study of American values that shape public policy, Fowler states, "equal opportunity has always been a major value in U.S. education policy" (2000, 113). J. R. Lucas adds, "Equality is the great political issue of our time. The demand for equality obsesses all our political thought. We are not sure what it is . . . but we are sure that whatever it is, we want it" (1997, 104). Monk defines equity as the "fairness in the distribution of some good, service, or burden" (1990, 35), but because equity is so difficult to measure, even he admits that a fair distribution can include substantial elements of inequality.

Though equity has been a rallying cry for American policy since the Declaration of Independence held "these truths to be self evident, that all men are created equal," the application of that truth has always been a little vague. Lampman (1977) maintains that equity, like beauty, is in the eye of the beholder. Most Americans agree that education is important to give all children a chance to succeed, but they usually want their own children's chances to be a little more equal (Cohen and Neufeld 1981).

The roots of American educational equity can be traced back to Andrew Jackson's concepts about education, formed between 1820 and 1840. Jackson viewed public education as the great leveler to provide a common base for building a cohesive society. For this reason, it was important that education be free for all. He rejected all of the aristocratic patterns of European education and embraced an equality of access for everyone. According to Jackson, all people could take—and should have the opportunity to take—leadership roles (Zimmerman 1997). The common school movement articulated by Horace Mann from 1839 to 1852 brought education to the masses. Before the emergence of the common school movement, secondary education in America was a privilege of select youth, usually males, and was provided by private schools and academics (Carlson 1996).

In the nineteenth century, equity took the form of providing each child with access to elementary school. As the twentieth century progressed, it was expanded to secondary education, and in the last forty years we have seen the ideal of equity lead to education policies designed to improve the access of minority children, girls, and the handicapped to various portions of the school program (Fowler 2000). The Civil Rights Movement of the 1950s, 1960s, and 1970s has touched all aspects of schooling. From requiring schools to desegregate to the development of magnet schools (voluntary segregation—the beginning of school choice) to the multicultural movement of the 1980s, schools have been forced to reform through equity legislation (Spring 1994). Equity is primarily concerned with the rights of individuals or groups of people, and experts predict it will continue to be a driver of change well into the twenty-first century (Verstegen 1994).

However, even with legislation designed to provide equity, in reality, many of the schools in America's poorest urban areas still suffer desperately from insufficient resources, decaying buildings, students and teachers in crisis, disintegrating communities, lack of opportunities, and funding systems that seem to continue to widen the gap between the poor and the affluent (Kozol 1991; White 1993).

The U.S. Supreme Court's decision in *Brown v. Board of Education* in 1954 put equity at the center stage of the education debate, and even though strides were made through the 1964 Civil Rights Act and the Elementary and Secondary Education Act of 1965, substantial inequities in educational opportunities still existed. Although schools were not allowed to segregate children by race, there were still vast inequities between rich and poor districts. Students were not receiving an equal education (Firestone et al. 1997). The harsh reality of inequity that exists in public schools was best expressed by Kozol (1991) in *Savage Inequalities,* which documents the remarkable degree of racial and economic segregation (and inherent inequity) that persists in the United States.

THE PRESSURE OF EQUITY

Some districts and states have attempted to achieve equity through a system of choice. One of the first attempts took place in Minneapolis in 1971 through a program called the Southeast Alternatives Project. This project gave parents and teachers a choice of four different kinds of schools: a traditional school, a modified "open" school, a continuous progress school, and a K–12 "free" school. By 1976 this approach to desegregation was so popular, it had been adopted by the Minneapolis school board as the city's systemwide desegregation remedy (Clinchy 1992).

School choice was introduced into public education in this country primarily as a means to achieve peaceful desegregation. School policies to desegregate reflect *Brown v. Board of Education* and the value of equity; however, in recent years many educators and parents have seen choice as one of the most powerful means to achieve significant changes and improvements in the quality of education offered in our public schools (Clinchy 1992).

The movement to provide equity reached persons with disabilities in the late 1960s when the Education of All Handicapped Children Act was signed into law. This law made the public legally responsible for providing free and appropriate education for all children (Sagor 1999). However, changing what seemed (in the minds of the majority) to be successful schools in the 1960s and 1970s was not a high priority for the public at large. As a result, there was an increase in the creation of separate alternatives for those who wanted or needed to be educated outside of the mainstream. Many of these new "alternative schools" became separate but unequal systems, attracting disenfranchised students who were already on trajectories of failure (Sagor 1999).

Reviewing the history of special education over the last forty years provides insight into the development of equity within the educational system. When federal law required special education for disabled students, most schools developed well-funded programs that met the technical requirements of the law, but generally those programs were located in separate rooms and sometimes even separate buildings. Many "special education" students had little contact with general education students or teachers (Sagor 1999).

The trend of parents to exercise choice by not sending their children to public schools has grown quietly over the last thirty years; recently, it has reached a point where educators are taking notice. The increase of private schools, home schools, virtual schools, and charter schools has shown a clear pattern. If Americans perceive that they are in a situation that is not equitable or of poor quality, they will do everything within their power to change that situation—including leaving the system, if necessary. According to Stull and Ryan (2000), the number of home-schooled children in the United States is increasing rapidly, and its growth is a reflection of the current wave of discontent with public education. In 1985, there were an estimated 50,000 homeschoolers. Ten years later, the number was somewhere between 500,000 and 750,000. Charter schools and private schools have shown similar patterns of exponential growth over the last decade (Stull and Ryan 2000).

Although a growing number of individuals have been seeking equity solutions outside of the mainstream system since the 1970s, reformers have attempted to bring equity into the system through efficiency or funding formulas. To level the playing field between schools, districts, and states across the country, advocates of equity have argued for equal funding under the equal protection clause of the U.S. Constitution.

However, in 1973 the Supreme Court voted 5–4 in *San Antonio v. Rodriguez* that because education was not mentioned in the U. S. Constitution, it was not a fundamental right that must be provided equally to all students. The battle was then taken to the states. State courts were inundated with pleadings alleging violations of the education and equal-protection clauses of state constitutions. As a result, state legislatures have reformed their school finance systems. Between 1970 and 1980 alone, twenty-eight states enacted new or revised education aid programs with the goal of financial equity. Twelve of these reforms were in direct response to court cases (Firestone et al. 1997).

Lawsuits have been the most effective way of advancing school financial equity because they appeal to the deep-seated equity value most Americans possess. As a result, the share of state education expenditures nationwide rose from 40 percent in 1970 to nearly 50 percent in 1986, where it has since leveled off (Statistics 1995). The increase is a direct result of increased equity legislation during that period.

Berne and Stiefel (1984) discuss three kinds of equity: horizontal equity, vertical equity, and equal opportunity. *Horizontal equity* is the equal treatment of equals. This principle states that students who are equal should be treated as such. In terms of financial equity, very often states treat all students as equal when it comes to funding formulas. The problem with horizontal equity is that it is easily refuted. People are not the same, and hence are not equal. In funding formulas, some states make adjustments based on whether a student is an English-language learner (ELL), pregnant, or at-risk in some other way.

Vertical equity is the unequal treatment of unequals. This principle recognizes the fact that people are different and advocates that students who are unequal should receive appropriately unequal treatment. The flaw with vertical equity is in identifying legitimate differences that should be accounted for. Often these differences fall along value lines. For instance, people are in general agreement that learning disabilities are a difference that deserves unequal treatment. However, there is great debate on whether differences of sex, religion, race, poverty, and ethnicity, for example, constitute a need for unequal treatment or vertical equity.

The final equity domain, *equal opportunity*, is assessed with respect to income, wealth, region of the country, and race. A question of equal opportunity would look at the correlation between income and the opportunity for someone to receive a quality education. In a system that falls short of equal opportunity, wealth or race would have a positive or negative effect on a person's ability to receive a quality education. These disparities are a function of equity. In a system that has strong levels of equal opportunity, everyone has an equal chance to succeed regardless of race, religion, or how much money they have.

According to Johns, Morphet, and Alexander (1983), equality of opportunity for all does not mean that every student has the same program of education. Nor does it mean that all students have the same amount of money expended on them. Rather, it means that every person should have the opportunity for the kind and quality of education that will best meet his or her needs as an individual and member of society.

Berne's definitions can be traced to Aristotle's thoughts on equality. According to Aristotle, equality was the same treatment for similar persons, but he also understood that though two people might be similar in some respects, they are different in most others. Therefore, his notion of justice was the unequal treatment of unequals (Patterson 1978). Treatment should be according to need—very much similar to the idea of equal opportunity.

Although equity means different things to different people, the notion of equity elicited one common element in the interviews with principals. In general, principals do not primarily see equity as equal treatment. They view equity as equal opportunity and strive to make their schools places where all students have an opportunity to reach their full potential:

> Equity is opportunities where each student has an opportunity to be learning and achieving at his or her best. It does not mean equal. I would base it more on needs that are in the students rather than "here is something that everybody gets." I don't believe in the same treatment

for everybody—I don't think that is equitable and that is not always understood.—*medium-sized rural high school*

Equity is not the same for all. It is doing what is best for all—not being the
same. It is providing opportunities according to student need and available
resources. Resources maintain quality, and quality equals equity.—*large
urban high school*

Principals were in strong support of equal opportunity and often
mentioned it in their definitions of equity:

Equity is providing the same opportunities for all people, regardless of
their race, ethnicity, disability, and social economic status, but it even
goes farther than that—for some students you have to offer even more
because they don't come to school with the same assets, education, and
socioeconomic advantages as others. It is providing them with whatever
it takes to bring them up to the same level as their peers—like the breakfast program, everyone has the opportunity for breakfast.—*large urban
middle school*

Equity is when every student has equal opportunity and if any student
wants to pursue an activity, interest, or program in the school, they know
they will be considered on their skills and demonstrated competencies,
not on anything else.—*large suburban high school*

EQUAL OPPORTUNITY THROUGH THE
MEETING OF NEEDS

The concept of equal opportunity was a major driver behind special-
education policy in the 1960s. Equality of opportunity is the removal of
every obstacle to the fulfillment of the individual—whether prejudice,
or ignorance, or treatable physical impairment. It means those without
status or wealth or membership in a privileged group will have full access of opportunity (Gardner 1984). Mort, Reusser, and Polley defined
equality of educational opportunity as "a principle that is fundamental
in American education—a principle based upon the assumption that our
democracy is best served by extending to all children an equal minimum

opportunity to attend schools adequate for the achievement of self-real-
ization, economic efficiency, civil efficiency and efficiency in human relationships" (1960, 19).

Equity can be defined in terms of need. Richard Lavoie, executive
director of the Riverview School in the town of Sandwich, Massachusetts, states that equity does not mean that everyone gets the same
treatment but instead that everyone gets what he or she needs (Sullo
1997). The objective of the standards movement itself—to successfully
educate all children, rich and poor, to the same high standard—is revolutionary. Equity lies in giving each child what he or she needs to
reach and exceed those standards (Chase 2000). Standards are the
road to equity, and they are crucial to reducing the educational inequalities that have affected many American families for decades
(Murnane 2000).

Principals agree that meeting needs is a strong component of equity,
whether that need is socioeconomic, academic, or relationship-based:

> Meeting needs is a huge a part of equity—realizing that different people
> have a different set of needs and different level of needs, and just because
> you have to give more to one person does not mean that you are not be-
> ing equitable to another population. It is just saying that you realize that
> this population is not coming to this school with the same language skills
> with the same socioeconomic skills that another group comes here with.
> If you help get them up to these standards, then at least they are equipped
> to go from here with the skills they need to be successful.—*large urban
> middle school*

> I think equity is the opportunity to give a person the time they need at
> a given moment. Let me explain. I tell the faculty there are times I will
> spend more time with each and every one of you. You might think, "hey,
> he is not spending time with me" or "he is being cold," I explain to them
> that your time will come. Sometimes, I tell the faculty that I will spend
> 20 minutes on a 30-second discipline referral because I want to build a
> relationship with that student so that I can use it in the future and make
> a connection. The whole thing is connections here. Everything is built
> on relationships and the group has bought into that. So, to answer your
> question, equity is based building proper relationships at a given time.—
> *small rural high school*

CONCLUSION

Everyone wants to be fair. No one wants to be accused of being unjust. For this reason, many people make a living defending and accusing others of being unjust. Laws are passed and policies are developed that continually seek to provide equity. When it comes to managing schools, principals do not see fairness—treating everyone the same—as the priority. The priority is meeting student needs—that much is clear. The question becomes how to help stakeholders understand that priority, discover ways to accurately determine needs, and somehow marshal dwindling resources to meet them.

Discussion Points

1. How would you define equity?
2. What value does equity play as a driver of policy and change in your school or district?
3. How do your clients (students and parents) define equity?
4. How do the teachers in your system define equity?
5. In what ways do you determine the needs of your students? Parents? Teachers?

4

THE POWER OF EFFICIENCY

This is the worst I have seen in budgets. I was in California when they went through budget crisis, but it was nothing like this. Then I went to Texas when they had the robin-hood laws, but nothing like this. That was nothing like this. You knew in the past you always had a little money for flex room. If you save a little bit here, and then a little bit there, you get that six or seven hundred dollars you need for a class or a major project. There is no six or seven hundred dollars. I am down to pennies . . . we are at that breaking point. The problem right now is we are working too many people too much. And we can't get more efficient right now.—*small rural high school*

EFFICIENCY DEFINED

Efficiency is obtaining the best-possible return on an expenditure or investment. It relates to the desire to get the largest benefit from any spending (Hanushek et al. 1994). In a capitalist society, efficiency is an important value and has major implications for policymaking and legislation. It has been the major driver for change in the corporate world (White 2001). It also has great influence in the realm of education. An educational system is efficient when it achieves high levels of student learning with relatively low expenditures of resources. Resources are not just the dollar figure spent on educating kids, but what those dollars buy—time, materials, services, and pace of instruction (Stockard and Mayberry 1992). At every government level, policymakers are concerned about how much education costs and whether certain reforms and improvement efforts are worth the cost (Fowler 2000).

Researcher Eric Hanushek chaired a panel of thirteen economists for a period of four years (1989–1993) whose mission was to bring economic thinking to the reform of American schools. The panel saw evidence of pervasive inefficiencies within the educational system and maintained that history suggests spending money on effective programs will not naturally or automatically happen in the current structure of schools. The panel saw no reason to believe that increases in spending would be any more effective than past spending and identified three key policy principles that are essential to improving the efficiency of U.S. schools: Resources devoted to education must be used efficiently; improved performance incentives must be introduced in schools; and changes must be based on systematic experimentation and evaluations of what does and does not work (Hanushek et al. 1994).

In the last thirty years, three streams of research have shaped our thinking about efficiency. This research has focused on how much money is spent on education, whether money makes a difference in student performance, and whether money is spent wisely (Firestone et al. 1997).

Education Costs Over Time

Research about the amount of money spent on education has shown that the cost of education has grown since the turn of the century—even when adjusted for inflation and changes in student enrollment (Hanushek et al. 1994). Depending on the decade, the national per-pupil cost of education has changed dramatically. In the 1960s, spending increased 69 percent. In the 1970s, there was a 35 percent increase, and the 1980s also saw a 35 percent increase. The 1990s and early 2000s have shown relatively flat spending on education. The increases during the 1960s and 1970s were a direct result of implementing equity legislation (Firestone et al. 1997).

The Effect of Increased Spending on Achievement

The second domain of research regarding efficiency focuses on whether increased spending makes a difference in student performance. In this area, the research is conflicting. Coleman et al. (1966) were the first to systematically document the impact of nonschool conditions, especially family background, on student learning. An extensive body of research has since developed that has attempted to identify a "production function" that would spell out the inputs that contribute to student achievement (Firestone et al. 1997). Research in this tradition has clearly demonstrated the strong effects of individual background on student learning. However, the degree to which financial inputs can overcome the effects of family background has been hotly debated, and analysts disagree on how to interpret the same studies (Natriello, McDill, and Pallas 1990). There have been many studies that indicate no relationship or very small associations between greater expenditures and students' achievement. However, it is important to note that when a significant relationship does appear, it is usually in the direction of increased student achievement resulting (at least indirectly) from increased expenditures. (Stockard and Mayberry 1992).

Johns, Morphet, and Alexander (1983) maintain that when the quantity or the quality of education is increased, financial support needs to be increased as well. When financial support is restricted, the quantity and quality of education are likely to diminish. They also maintain that it is easier to see a direct relationship between quantities of educational resources and finances than quality of education. More books will cost more money. Hiring more teachers will increase expenses. However, when it comes to the quality of education as related to cost, there is a wide difference of opinion. Many people would agree that increasing the quality is likely to add to the cost. Fewer agree that increasing the cost necessarily results in better quality, and most people agree that many gains in quality can be attained without increasing costs.

Johns, Morphet, and Alexander admit quality is difficult to measure because it can be defined in so many ways. However, on the basis of numerous studies, they reached the following conclusion regarding quality:

> The quality of education provided in school systems where expenditures are low is far less satisfactory than that in systems where expenditures are

above the nation average. Low expenditures tend to result in inadequate leadership, large classes, poor teachers and teaching, and other features that contribute to low quality. (1983, 184)

How Districts Spend Their Money

The third line of research regarding efficiency examines how districts spend their money—paying particular attention to the amount of money directed to the classroom and the instruction of students. The assumption is that focusing resources at the classroom level increases efficiency. These studies have shown that, regardless of size, districts spend their resources in similar ways: About 60 to 70 percent of budgets go to instruction, and another 8 to 10 percent on instructional supports (student services, curriculum development, and professional development). Administrative costs count for around 10 percent of budgets (Odden et al. 1995). Some state report cards attempt to show how much districts are spending on services in relation to each other. Such information on the report cards is a product of our accountability culture and a reflection of our desire for an efficient use of resources.

HOW PRINCIPALS VIEW EFFICIENCY

The principals interviewed see efficiency not only as the amount of resources available to achieve the goals of their school but also as an effective use of those resources. They define resources as time, money, materials, and services. Because the interviews were conducted during an unprecedented time of dwindling financial resources, all of the respondents were feeling the pressure of the need to be efficient. The majority of principals stated that 2003 was the worst year they had ever seen in Oregon when it came to financial resources, and most had deep concerns for the future of public education and how it is financed:

There is more pressure and accountability. Before property tax reductions, if we had a problem, you would just throw money at it. We saw results. When a school was struggling with reading, we hired a specialist, and did a school-wide in-service and saw reading scores increase. We are moving from educating students to warehousing them—standardization has helped all students to read and write but we are losing kids in different ways.—*large urban high school*

When it comes to time efficiency and the cutbacks, you know I am not working any harder than I was last year. Very conservatively, we work 65 hours a week and through the winter we work 75 to 80 hours a week and every weekend. You can't work any more, so the question becomes what are you going to prioritize. You have to think, "what do I have to give up and what can I not feel guilty about?" Everything has meaning. Some things have more meaning than others. From the leadership point of view, I am really insistent on focus. So knowing we can't do it all, what are we going to focus on and what is an absolutely priority?—*large suburban high school*

I'm just cutting back, department by department. Efficiency is not something I am on the cutting edge of. One thing we have done is stop purchasing new technology because the bang for your buck with new technology is not commensurate with the amount it costs. We just can't afford it anymore. That gives me great fear, because in two or three years, all of this is going to be obsolete. As you can see this 1997 computer—it's getting bad.—*large suburban high school*

We are hurting. Next year, I am going to have to eliminate some programs and class size is going to be bigger and class sizes are going to be in the mid-30s, and when you do these hands-on projects, the efficiency is just not there. You are going to do less of the activities because it takes more time to get 35 kids through it than 28. That is the real panic to me. We've spent a good five years, especially the last principal, really building a strong program and I am going to see it dismantle a little bit here.— *medium-sized rural high school*

STRATEGIES FOR IMPROVING FINANCIAL EFFICIENCY

There are many ways to improve an educational system's efficiency, but they all fall into three categories (Coombs and Hallak 1972). Efficiency may be improved by changing the amounts, quality, or proportions of inputs (teachers, students, instructional materials, curriculum, facilities, equipment, and supplies) without changing the system's existing form. Modifying the system's basic design dramatically can also increase efficiency. This involves the introduction of new components and technology (online coursework, video conferencing, computers, etc.). The third, more radical approach to improving efficiency would be to design a brand new alternative teaching and learning system that differs dramatically from the present one.

In some places around the country, the third approach is exactly what is happening. The rise of students in private schools, charter schools, for-profit schools, online schools, homeschools, and a host of other alternative schools is evidence of people looking for new efficiencies when it comes to the education of children.

Policymakers have adopted three strategies to improve the financial efficiency of schools. The first involves a continued focus on better management practices that are being used in business circles. The second strategy is tied to restricting the amount states can spend on education through tax-limitation policies. Nearly all states impose some type of limitation on school taxes and/or spending, or revenues (Firestone et al. 1997).

The third approach is accountability. By tying accountability systems (a measure of excellence) to efficiency, states are developing ways to measure student performance (generally standardized tests and other performance assessments) and then developing policies to use the student outcome data to develop school improvement plans and generate financial rewards and sanctions (Firestone et al. 1997). Such a system links together efficiency and excellence. Schools become accountable to use their resources in ways that will lead to improved student learning outcomes.

CONCLUSION

The argument for adequate and equitable funding is clear. "As a society, we cannot skimp on educational resources and expect our schools to be effective. Teachers and students deserve adequate resources and they deserve to have these equitably distributed" (Stockard and Mayberry 1992, 121). But the questions remain, what is the right amount, and what would be the result of using that amount? Principals of public schools—at this time more than any other—are looking for ways to become more efficient. The next breakthrough in school improvement will come in the form of schools and districts becoming more efficient with their resources: time, money, and materials.

Discussion Points

1. In what ways has your school or district struggled with the pressures associated with trying to achieve efficiency?
2. In what ways has your organization become more or less efficient?
3. When efficiency becomes the priority, what happens to equity and excellence?
4. How can you demonstrate the power of efficiency in your school or district?

5

SURVIVING THE
TRIANGLE OF TENSION

I have an absolutely unshakeable belief that we are the cornerstone of a democratic society. This is the most important profession on earth, and I will argue anyone until I am blue in the face because I believe that. I believe that 20 to 40 years from now, we will look back and view the work that we do as heroic. The challenges that we face are greater than are faced in any other profession and our commitment to children and outcomes for children are more significant than any other work bar none—so that is what keeps me going.— *large suburban high school*

The triangle of tension boils down to one word—accountability, and it is accountability to excellence, equity, and efficiency that principals must face on a daily basis. Accountability, however, is nothing new.

A CULTURE OF ACCOUNTABILITY

The need for educators to be accountable to their public has existed as long as parents have been sending their children to school. Over 2,000 years ago, Plutarch wrote, "Fathers, themselves, ought every few days to test their children, and not rest their hopes on the disposition of a hired teacher; for even those persons will devote more attention to the children if they know they must from time to time render an account" (Ulich 1948, 96).

Because the family was the first educational institution, parents were accountable for the instruction of their children. As clans, tribes, and states developed, the functions of education became more formalized and the fortunes of the clans, tribes, and states were more or less determined by the performance of the educational system that was established (Morris 1972).

Although the form of accountability has varied over time, the end product—performance—has remained constant. However, the accountability responsibility extends beyond the students. It also includes informing constituencies about performance and implies responding to feedback (Cunningham 1972).

Accountability is a concern about output, and in the United States reformers have been devising ways to scientifically measure educational outputs for over 100 years. "Beginning at least as early as 1883, many individuals, committees, and commissions have examined the U.S. educational system and found it wanting" (Bracey 1994, 1). Horace Mann, an early nineteenth-century school reformer, got into a conflict with Boston schoolmasters over the quality of education in the schools, and he was able to persuade the local school communities to administer uniform written exams to a sample of students. The results of the exams supported his criticisms, and Mann's new evaluation technique was not adopted (Wynne 1972).

In 1883, Joseph Mayer-Rice looked at public schools and found them lacking in supervision, filled with untrained teachers, and controlled by politically corrupt boards (Bracey 1994). By 1895, Rice was able to persuade schools to administer a spelling test to 16,000 students. The results of the test showed no correlation between the amount of time schools spent on spelling lessons and the achievement of the students. However, the results were widely criticized by educators, who were united in denouncing how foolish it was to try to discover the value of teaching by whether or not students could spell on a test. They claimed the object of such work was not to teach children how to spell but to develop their minds (Wynne 1972).

Rice, a pediatrician with training in psychological measurement, didn't stop there. In 1902 he published an article in *The Forum*, a journal of social criticism, about the need for school accountability. He criticized educators for basing the structure of education on a foundation of opinions and called for using scientific methods of measurement to determine what methods of teaching and schooling were most effective. Rice established a department of education research through *The Forum* but could never implement his research plans because of a lack of funds and the hostility of educators (Wynne 1972). Rice was pressing for a measure of quality, but finances (a function of efficiency and illustration of the triangle of tension) hindered his excellence movement.

Although educators were able to frustrate accountability efforts from the research community, they could not avoid the management efficiency model of Fredrick Taylor, which was sweeping through the business community in the early twentieth century (Wynne 1972). Similar to our current standards movement, this was another example of schools reflecting the trends of society, not determining them (Patterson 1978).

In an application of the scientific management principles of Taylorism, administrators focused on the rate of student promotion through grades or the time spent in various classes as indicators of efficiency. Rather than measure outputs—what students were learning—they zeroed in on inputs—what students were exposed to—in an attempt to measure efficiency. Educators of the day were not fond of the effects of Taylorism on schools, and that attitude persists today (Wynne 1972).

The Birth of Standardized Testing

The first major breakthrough in the standardized test movement came as a result of World War I. Behavioral psychologists were employed to advise the Army on ways to classify and identity the talents of millions of draftees. Their recommendations involved the large-scale adoption of objective, uniform tests. Schools soon followed suit and began using standardized tests as a means to measure student ability and aptitude (Wynne 1972). The tests have changed over the years and are under constant revision, but the basic purpose of testing has been to measure individual student performance rather than school performance. Only in the last few years have standardized tests been used to measure overall school performance, and there is sill great disagreement among school reformers about whether these standardized tests are accurate measures of the effectiveness of teachers and the learning of students (Kohn 1999).

As some researchers have noted (Porter 1994), the tendency in the United States to hold students accountable for their achievement but not hold schools accountable for what they produce is odd, but we are on the verge of seeing that trend change. The recent implementation of the No Child Left Behind Act is an early indicator of accountability measures to come, and the reaction of educators across the nation mirrors the reaction of our counterparts a hundred years ago: We still don't like outsiders judging us, telling us what to do, or holding us accountable.

The Importance of Accountability

Winch (1996) argues that any healthy system of education needs to maintain accountability. He declares that an organization is able to achieve accountability if it is possible to determine whether it fulfills the purpose for which it was set up. In other words, for accountability to operate, the purposes of the institution must be stated or at least agreed to by the interested parties. In the accountability debate, studies have shown that teacher quality is the leading factor in determining student achievement—even more important than economic conditions (Kelleher 2000). For this reason, energy, resources, and policies by state departments in recent years have been directed at teacher education and preparation programs in an attempt to produce more highly qualified teachers through a combination of higher standards, accountability, and expectations for new teachers.

The trend in recent years worldwide has been an increased range of accountability pressure not only from outside agencies but also from within the system through increased leadership responsibilities. Most nations have endeavored to decentralize some measure of authority, responsibility, and accountability to the school level while at the same time determining centralized standards frameworks that must be followed. There exists, therefore, "a paradox of simultaneous centralization and decentralization" (Caldwell and Spinks 1998, 11). This paradox increases the pressure on administrators to manage both the external demands of accountability and the internal increased responsibility demands that arise from having greater authority to act and make decisions.

Accountability is the degree to which students, staff, or parents take responsibility for their own progress toward achieving excellence, equity, and efficiency in their schools. Accountability pressure in the realm of excellence can come from a school board or superintendent because of low test scores. A principal must answer to financial accountability with the district business manager who, in turn, answers to the state, which has extensive policies regarding the proper use of school finances. And finally, the building principal is held accountable by parents, from investigating harassment reports, to class placement, to even their child's ultimate success. Needless to say, all that accountability adds up to a great deal of tension for school principals to manage.

Before the last decade, teachers and principals could meet the demands for accountability by simply working hard and following accepted professional standards. However, the current accountability movement emphasizes results, and experts have identified five essential elements in today's accountability systems: Rigorous contents standards are established; student progress is tested; professional development is aligned with standards and test results; results are publicly reported; and results lead to rewards, sanctions, and targeted assistance (Lashway 1999).

Christopher Winch (1996) argues that three historical pressures of accountability are currently affecting both policy and practice in education. The first pressure relates to the fact that people put their hopes in education. Even if these hopes are sometimes exaggerated, the fact remains that society views education as necessary to provide moral order and economic growth. The second pressure comes from the rise of neoliberalism in the United States. Neoliberals believe that the role of government should be kept to a minimum and that wherever possible, both public and private goods should be provided by the market. It is in this way that both freedom of choice and quality of service are ensured. The third accountability factor has been an overall decline in the deference toward professional people on the part of the general public. The combination of these three factors has put accountability in the forefront of the educational frontier.

HOW PRINCIPALS SUCCESSFULLY NAVIGATE THE TRIANGLE

Public school principals are remarkable people. In the face of seemingly insurmountable problems, they rise again and again to the challenge and find a way where there is no way. The principals I interviewed continually demonstrated their innovative nature and resilience to not only survive the triangle of tension but even use its accountability demands to generate school improvement.

Excellence: Standards-Based Instruction

The principals I interviewed felt pressure in the transformation from content-driven instruction to standards-based instruction. However, in nearly all cases, this tension was viewed as a positive step toward excellence because it improved instruction:

> The good part of school reform has been helping us find the targets. Setting the standards is not a bad thing. Especially in my previous school experience, it created a sense of urgency to make sure we were teaching to the standards.—*large suburban high school*

> Initially, I would suggest that on the front end it gave us a framework for improvement, some pretty good targets. And I am invested in those targets. I want all of my kids to be competent readers. I want all of my kids to have math skills throughout their lifetime. I am fully committed to the standards as they were initially adopted.—*large suburban high school*

> They [the standards] have definitely made us focus on making our children learn all the content they need to succeed on state achievement tests. We have a very strong focus on getting our curriculum aligned and adopting new textbooks as they come along that we think the kids will be successful with, so we seek more and more of those opportunities as a result of that pressure.—*large suburban middle school*

> I think our department leaders handle that tension pretty darn well—our math department especially. They rallied to the cause, looked at the standards, compared them to the national standards, planned the curriculum

around that, and held people accountable to what they agreed to do—so I think that standards-based instruction has pretty good support here.—*large suburban high school*

There was more tension at the beginning making the transition to standards, but as far as now, that tension is minimal at this point.—*medium-sized rural high school*

Innovations Related to Excellence   Some principals increased the achievement or excellence of their school through innovations that improved instruction or the school climate in some way. In many instances, those innovations took a great deal of time and energy to implement:

I wanted to implement an advisory period and divide the students into groups of 20 to 25 and have the teachers be responsible for one group and they monitor their academic success and whether they were on track to meet the Certificate of Initial Mastery [performance-based assessment certificate issued by high schools in Oregon]. It took me a year to get that program implemented. We attended the national middle school conference. We attended the Turning Points 2000 conference. We bought books for the site council about it. We developed a matrix that showed what we are doing, what Turning Points 2000 suggests we do, and what we need to do. After we did that, I kept the charts up where people could see them, and by the end of the year, I convinced people that we needed an advisory period. As a result of that, we have an advisory that meets daily by grade level in alphabetical order and they meet with the same teacher for three years, but it was not something that I could just start—the biggest part was allowing them to be a part of the learning process and not just shoving the decision on their backs, so that they actually owned the decision. We had to have 85 percent approval by the teachers and we got it.—*large urban middle school*

A year ago, we got school improvement funds from the state. With those funds we ran a full-time reading position. We had a dynamite secondary reading teacher. I sat down with her in the summer and we analyzed the 8th-grade reading scores, and we created target populations of kids, groups of 15, that were similarly skilled, and we really built them up. It was kind of a glorified Title program at a high school. I know the research says you can't do that at the high school level, but you can, and you can be effective.

We had our largest jump in reading scores ever, we went from 52 percent to 62 percent of students meeting standards and the number of kids just barely below standard was huge as well. There was an enormous shift in reading performance in one year.—*large suburban high school*

Core knowledge is an application of excellence because it defines what a student needs to know and helps teachers organize their curriculum and content. Core knowledge is content driven and the standards are taught within the required content. Students leave knowing certain basic things. That's important.—*medium-sized rural K–8*

Right now we are into the senior projects and I have dived into them more this year than any other year, and it is just amazing to see these kids. Some are in total panic mode right now, but others have done phenomenal work all year, and that is what it is about. For those involved in the senior project, it becomes a part of their year-end demonstration. What they have done in those senior projects absolutely blows your socks off.—*medium-sized rural high school*

I would share with you that we are engaging meaningful experiences for kids in some real nontraditional avenues. We surveyed our kids and asked them what they liked and what got them excited, and as a result of that, we started a rugby club, a swing dance club, a robotics club, an equestrian club that we have never had before and the participation is great. And you know that when kids are participating in things, they are engaged in school and do much better.—*large suburban high school*

Providing Equity

Depending on the situation, principals think of equity in two different ways: equal treatment and equal opportunity. Equal treatment refers to fairness: treating everyone the same. However, the majority of the time, principals strive to create equal opportunity. In a school system that provides equal opportunity, some students are provided unequal (or additional) resources so that they may have an equal opportunity to achieve success. The fact that school districts receive an additional 50 percent of basic state support for students with disabilities from the federal government is an example of how equal opportunity functions in finance formulas.

Equal Treatment   In the business of managing a school, principals worked hard to provide equality when it came to staffing, programming, equipment, and other resources:

> Look at academics. We have some veteran teachers who have been teach-ing for 18 years that don't want to give up calculus. We have a philosophy of share the wealth. We want more unified ownership of the students. You don't want someone to have only lower-level math, that doesn't make his or her job fun. It doesn't set them up for success or bring new life into the program. So how do we apply equity? We share the wealth. So no one gets all upper-division classes. Everyone has at least one, if not two.—*small ru-ral high school*

Many principals felt their schools are better places because of eq-uity policies that promote diversity, and the majority of principals ac-tively worked to ensure that all students are treated in an equitable manner:

> We have a student of the month and I watched the wall all last year and this year I got my advisory group out to look at the wall and tell me what they saw. They couldn't see it. I said, "We are a very diverse school. Do you see diversity reflected here?" I told them that we have to get the word out—a black kid, an Asian kid, a Hispanic kid can be student of the month. Now, how are we going to tell that to the staff? When my kids go walking through the building, I don't want them thinking you have to be white to be student of the month.—*large urban middle school*

Equal Opportunity to Achieve Success   Principals sought ways to develop programs that will meet the equity needs of their students, and even in the midst of dwindling resources, principals still tried to provide equal opportunities for their students and defined those oppor-tunities according to need. Principals looked for ways to meet student needs primarily through differentiating instruction and developing com-prehensive programs:

> Students do have different needs. ELL students need more time and in-struction with English and kids with special education needs are going to need some additional differentiated instruction.—*large suburban high school*

If a teacher has less students to get to know and work with on a daily basis, they are able to differentiate their instruction more, so with a caseload
of 90 students a semester rather than 180, they can get to know their students well, know their work well, know their learning style well, and meet
their needs accordingly. As they meet their needs, excellence is a result.
The block schedule facilitates that kind of relationship building.—*large
urban high school*

Let me tell you about another one. I met with a consultant from the ESD
[regional educational service center] and talked about the needs of my
growing ELL population. He came to me and said, "I know we could
never have this, but I am asking for a room in the middle of the school
where the kids could have their own homeroom—a place to hang out."
We created a space for them. They can decorate it any way they want and
determine when they get to go there. So am I treating all kids like that?
No, I am not, but for my ELL kids to be invested in school, that is what
they needed.—*large suburban high school*

We provide opportunities for at-risk kids and programs that try to meet
student needs at their own rate and level of learning. They are not great,
but they are pretty good programs, and despite our budget cuts, we have
maintained those programs. I think some of the federal laws, especially
around equity, have pushed some organizations, including our own, to
provide more opportunities for all people. I think federal laws and policies have facilitated that.—*large suburban high school*

Principals were able to help shape the school climate to reflect equal
opportunity—especially when the climate was organized around student
need:

When I came on board here, we had an awful lot of people here who were
labeling kids, gang kids, punkers, etc. etc., and I kind of got on a plat-
form—this is based on a spiritual belief—that we have to practice to un-
conditional love and acceptance of every child, regardless of where they
come from or what they look like. We started with that point of view and
the commitment we are going to reach out to kids that are dropping out,
kids that are at-risk.—*large suburban high school*

It isn't the end result that makes a difference, but it is where you provide
hope. Every student, every period, every day should feel a sense of hope.

We implemented those philosophies and saw a dramatic increase in positive student behavior. Last year, out of 1186 students, we had a total of 6 students that had disciplinary actions for altercations—that's three fights all year. That's just unbelievable, particularly for freshman.—*medium-sized rural high school*

It goes back to the concept that every kid has to be valued when they walk into the building. We show them that they are valued—even if we don't agree with some of their opinions.—*large suburban high school*

Efficiency: Positive Effects

Principals have found a variety of ways to stretch their dwindling resources. Most of the efficiencies gained were seen in the area of resources or staff efficiencies. Resource gains are defined in terms of time, money, and materials:

The principals in my league up here, we get together once a month and brainstorm and share ideas. At the beginning, it was athletics, but in the last year and a half, we changed that—now we spend 90 percent of the time on academics. And that has helped immensely. We share handbooks, laws, and stories. That has saved us time so we are not reinventing the wheel. We have shared curriculum. We have actually shared textbooks, and we loaned them back and forth.—*small rural high school*

When I think of efficiency, I think of time . . . and my experience in the schools I have been at—which is contrary to what others say—is it is not the amount of time students are there, but the quality of time spent on instruction. I had one school that met just the minimum requirements in terms of time, but they were the highest-performing school in their demographics of anywhere in the state. It was a clear indicator that it wasn't the amount of time, it was the quality of the time that really counted. I look at research and I see how people emphasize the quality, not necessarily the quantity that has the biggest impact. Efficiency to me is being very clear about what it is you are doing every moment in a way that will benefit the kids instructionally.—*small rural K–8*

But I also learned we can get through it [budget reductions] and we were able to gain some more resources in a few years and hire some people back. And people in the community realized that we had taken a hit and they became more supportive and eventually, after many years of not passing a bond, they were able to pass a bond and now they are opening up a new high school this fall.—*large suburban high school*

What we have had to do now is move away from the general purchases and spend our money on the things that will really make a difference. Like supplies, we target our resources to meet the needs of specific students, and using our money to meet those needs. We target differentiated instruction and find the materials necessary to do that.—*small rural K–8*

One of the things we did in our second year here in order to get an efficient use of time in our staff meetings was to implement the concept of the Friday late starts. Our typical 30-minute staff meetings were not productive. We just didn't get anything done. Then we would go back and have all these things hanging over our heads. So, we went back to the school board and requested a two-hour late start every Friday, and they approved it. The amount of work that can be done is absolutely phenomenal. It goes from 7:30 to 9:30 and we just hit it, ready to go.—*medium-sized rural high school*

We have become more efficient with our time in a very purposeful manner from this office. My secretary and I have indulged in some very productive conversations about what it is we don't need to be doing and what it is we could be doing to be more helpful. We are eliminating some things we do at our award assembly by doing some things we think we can do in a better way that will be much more time efficient. One of the things we realize is how stressful August, September, and October is for us, so we have streamlined some of what we do there. We've spent less money because we have less money, but we have become more efficient in getting money from elsewhere.—*large suburban middle school*

Going to the 4 × 4 schedule was an efficiency move—it allows you to purchase less textbooks, and it also allows you build relationships with students on deeper levels because each teacher only works with 90 to 100 students a semester.—*large urban high school*

The budget reduction hasn't decreased our pursuit of excellence, but it has taken more personal toll, because we have to work harder and longer to get the same result. One of the ways we have facilitated that is by putting more and more things out there the staff can do to help. And they have really been remarkable in rising to the request.—*large suburban middle school*

We are doing more work with less people. We actually brought in an expert to work with the staff in the first week of January. I wrote to an author. He came and told us about working smarter and not harder. He gave us some nice efficiency concepts to work on. So, our school has become more efficient with less people.—*small rural high school*

It is our destiny to design the change we want. So, out of this something good can come. We can make sure we don't come back with the fat and programs we don't need. Before we add programs back, we are going to make sure they impact the key mission. So, there is a positive part—in addition, we can have a lot more integration. We are going to have a lot more integration next year then we have ever had before because it will be forced upon us. Our curriculum will be a lot more seamless because grades 7–12 will be joined together in one building.—*small rural high school*

Increased Support through Efficiency   Other principals remarked that going through tough budget decisions as a staff actually pulled people together to support each other to a greater degree than they had previously:

I guess having been in a district that was really hard hit, with 18 percent budget cuts before anyone else, we learned that there was a certain amount of creativity you can do, and sometimes, in the hard times, it pulls people together and creates a sense of community. A different response could occur, where people get defensive and negative and just say, "I am not going to do it," but that is when there is a call to leadership that says we are going to move forward given limited resources, whether through grants, extra effort, by volunteers, or partnerships with businesses.—*large suburban high school*

I have organized our youth pastors in the community. I told them we were losing an assistant principal and campus security. I asked them to set up their own rotating schedule and do lunch supervision for me. They set up a schedule, they all have IDs. They come in and help me out. We let them know about protocol around here, and they make positive connections with kids—it is another adult in the building making connections with kids and with those in their congregations.—*large suburban high school*

Positive efficiencies also came in the form of programs and policies from the state and federal levels. These included reform efforts and ways of assessment that lessen the impact of high-stakes testing:

At the budget committee meeting last night someone said they should get rid of the Certificate of Initial Mastery [statewide high school perform-ance assessment system in Oregon] in order to save money, and teachers stood up and said we wouldn't do anything different, the CIM isn't cost-ing us anything extra and it is improving instruction.—*medium-sized ru-ral high school*

We'd like to be able to test all along the way, and that is what TESA [Tech-nology Enhanced State Assessment] has allowed us to do. It has helped us to be able to test when children are ready.—*small rural K–8*

Going back to what lawmakers can do, I do think we need to look at a lot more consolidation of schools. I think NCLB is a hidden agenda to con-solidate schools. I don't care what you say—there shouldn't be schools that small if you can avoid it. We have a high school right down the road, 12 miles away from us. They went down to 2A this year. They are shrink-ing and their money is real tight—we can't even join up with them. But if legislators put in incentives to join, I think they would do it now. In the long run, they would save money everywhere.—*small rural high school*

CONCLUSION

Although principals have been successful at finding some solutions to balancing the demands of excellence, equity, and efficiency, there is still a great deal of tension and struggle associated with accountability to these values. Certainly, there are no easy answers or quick fixes to the triangle of tension. However, we can learn from the successes principals have experienced and apply that knowledge to designing a framework or model for successfully managing the triangle of tension. I have termed this model the *Quality School Improvement* (QSI) framework, and the next chapter is a discussion of this framework.

Discussion Points

1. How have the pressures of accountability affected your school or district?

2. Of the examples presented throughout this chapter, which is the most helpful to your school? Why?

3. Which value presents the greatest difficulty for you to manage: excellence, efficiency, or equity? Why?

4. After reading this chapter, do you have an efficiency, equity, or excellence idea you would like to try in your school?

6

QUALITY SCHOOL
IMPROVEMENT FRAMEWORK

Michael Fullan (2004) has identified raising the bar and closing the gap as the key priority driving change and improvement in education today. This is the primary work of educators—increasing achievement for all (raising the bar) and helping those who are underachieving reach their full potential (closing the gap). The excellence movement represents raising the bar, and the equity movement addresses closing the gap. Add the pressure to reduce costs and eliminate waste in public education, and you have another illustration of the triangle of tension at work.

Excellence. Equity. Efficiency. Do better. Be fair. Cut costs. These are the values driving the accountability movement in today's policy environment, and the triangle of tension they create for principals and school leaders at times seems almost insurmountable. From No Child Left Behind to Individuals with Disabilities Education Act (IDEA) to property tax limitations, school leaders find themselves caught in the crossfire between conflicting legislation. In the midst of shrinking budgets and expanding class sizes, closing the achievement gap while at the same time increasing achievement seems unrealistic, but there are places where this feat is being tackled head on. Researcher Michael Fullan documents that kind of achievement in his best-selling book, *The Moral Imperative of School Leadership* (2003).

RENEWAL, REFORM, AND RESTRUCTURING

Reformer and researcher David Conley (1999) designed a framework for understanding the activities associated with school improvement. In this framework, activities can be categorized as renewal, reform, or restructuring. *Renewal events* are school-improvement activities that help an organization run more efficiently but don't really change what the organization actually does or the way it functions.

Reform activities go deeper. They result in changing existing procedures and rules in an organization and help it adapt to changing circumstances. These changes are the result of external laws, policies, and pressures.

Restructuring involves activities that fundamentally change assumptions, practices, and relationships both within the organization and between the organization and the outside world. These changes lead to improvement and a variety of outcomes that benefit all students (Conley 1999).

The top-down school reforms of the 1980s generated changes in schools that were predominately external in nature. Schools and districts were forced to change because of the rise of new state and federal policies (Moses 1990). Restructuring represents the second wave of educational reform—longer lasting and more sustainable, but harder to implement. During the 1990s, basic improvements were seen in mathematics and literacy because teachers and principals were applying better knowledge, but many of these reforms lacked the ownership to make the changes sustainable (Fullan 2003). It is only through restructuring that schools can be re-created to close the achievement gap under an entirely new set of assumptions about purposes and practices.

TRUE EQUITY

True equity is based on need rather than treatment. In other words, true equity is not everyone receiving the same treatment, but everyone being treated according to their needs. In this way, equity and excellence can coexist; in fact, they are intricately linked to each other. The real question is not how these values compete for resources, but how re-sources can be distributed to support the cause of equity to achieve excellence.

Ford and Harmon (2001) questioned the notion that excellence and equity cannot coexist. They challenged the assumption that addressing the needs of equity results in diminishing levels of program quality. They recommend that to meet the needs of all students, those needs must be accurately determined through a variety of assessments beyond achievement tests. The work of Gardner (1983) and Sternberg (1985) has demonstrated that intelligence is multifaceted, complex, and manifests itself in many different ways. Practical, valid, reliable, and efficient ways to measure and determine the intelligence, learning style, and learning needs of students can be determined and applied by teachers working in unison.

Defining equity as the same treatment for all will not get us to excellence. If we think of equity according to individual student learning needs, we can begin designing efficient educational systems that seek to meet individual student needs rather than designing systems that seek to treat everyone the same.

Lloyd (2000) is an advocate for a complete redesign of how we educate students. He claims that providing excellence and equality of opportunity for all students cannot be done when the organization of schooling, the curriculum, and the assessment and testing procedures remain unchallenged—or unrestructured. He maintains that as long as the central energy in educational change is devoted to maintaining the status quo, inequality, and discrimination, the preclusion of excellence for all students will be the result—regardless of how much money is spent to achieve it.

There is a dilemma in balancing the educational demands of equity and excellence, and that balance cannot be achieved without moving away from an assembly-line concept of education in which all students receive the same instruction, curriculum, and interventions (Zimmerman 1997). To achieve this balance, there must be a shift to what Stevens calls a "quality-oriented paradigm" (1992, 50), in which equity is defined as equality of opportunity offered to each individual; excellence is achieved when an individual's specific needs are met and the individual can progress as far as his or her abilities allow.

QUALITY SCHOOL IMPROVEMENT

Excellence is continuous improvement compared to measurable results. It is the overall performance of the organization, the school grade, or the report card. Equity is the stepping-stone to excellence. The two are not in conflict; in fact, they are uniquely connected. The overall performance of the group will increase as the needs of the individual are met. When viewed as a system, equity and excellence are linked together. The goal is excellence, and equity is how you get there.

I have developed a framework that visually represents a way to manage the triangle of tension. A balance can be achieved between equity and excellence. In this framework, higher levels of efficiency result in higher levels of quality.

The framework begins with an arrow, as displayed in figure 6.1. If school leaders focus their energy on meeting the needs of their students and those working most closely with the instruction of the students (teachers), excellence—both individually for the student and collectively for the school—will be the result.

Resources (time, money, materials, and services) are finite. Each district and school is allotted a fixed amount. Figure 6.2 represents the allocation of resources. The equity–excellence arrow is placed according to resources received. For instance, an allocation of $4,000 per student would place the arrow lower on the resource bar than an allocation of $5000 per student.

Although finite resources are allocated to every school and district, schools do not use those resources in the same ways. How those resources are used is a function of efficiency. In this framework, efficiency of resources becomes the key to influencing the bar of excellence. As

Figure 6.1.   Equity has a direct affect upon excellence.

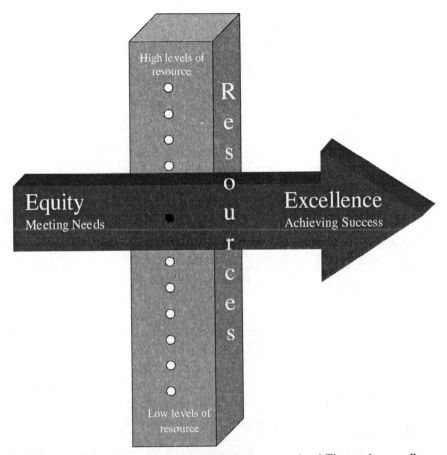

Figure 6.2.   Finite resources are allocated to every school. The equity-excellence arrow is placed according to the amount of resource received.

schools and districts become more effective at meeting needs, they are able to reach higher levels of quality without additional resources. Efficient schools are able to influence their equity–excellence arrow to achieve higher levels of quality, as demonstrated in figure 6.3.

MANAGING THE TRIANGLE OF TENSION

Excellence is personal. It is achieved when someone makes a commitment to continuous progress and becomes a learner. It is a battle that

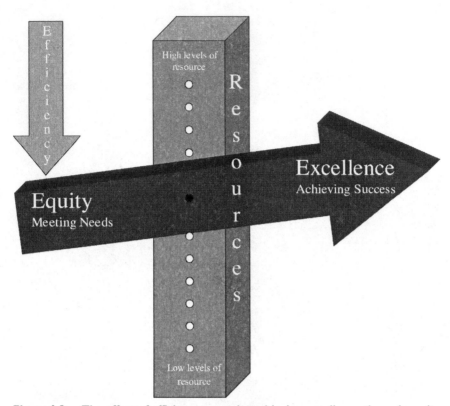

Figure 6.3. The effect of efficiency upon the achieving excellence through equity. The more efficient an organization is in meeting student needs, the higher levels of collective excellence will be achieved. Likewise, organizations that are inefficient at meeting needs will not achieve excellence. In this way, more efficient organizations are able to achieve greater excellence with fewer resources.

is won one person at a time—beginning with leadership. Equity is achieved by affecting the system. It requires organizational change, a new way of thinking that is focused on student need. It also requires the development of new structures and resources to support those structures. Efficiency is the means to achieve excellence through equity. Efficient organizations make the most of their resources: time, money, materials, and services. They have discovered ways to meet more needs with fewer resources than other organizations. Quality schools and districts have discovered not only how to manage the tension among excellence, equity, and efficiency but also how to use that tension to generate improvement.

To achieve quality, school leaders must rise above the control practices of accountability and strive for higher goals that require commitment and restructuring. By so doing, they will meet any and all demands generated by control agencies. The most effective way to reach high levels of quality is by meeting the instructional needs of the students and the professional needs of those who work with the students: teachers and staff members.

Equity is systemic. It is the responsibility of management to provide equity, so that all students have the opportunity to achieve success. Excellence is personal. It is the result of a choice, a decision, to take advantage of the opportunities afforded and achieve success. Quality schools use their resources effectively (efficiency) to achieve high levels of success (excellence) through the meeting of needs (equity).

ANALYZING QUALITY ACCORDING TO THE SCHOOL-IMPROVEMENT FRAMEWORK

The educational practices of the past have been based on the factory model, with an emphasis on mass production, following directions given by supervisors, and a tolerance for the completion of mind-dulling, repetitive tasks. With the advent of increased technology, automated machines and processes have pulled people off the assembly lines in America. More and more businesses need people who can think, problem solve, and run the machines that do the tedious work (Cramer 1996). Deming and Senge maintain that "85–95 percent of all problems are caused by the system" (Schenkat 1993, 9). In other words, the difficulties that we are facing in public education today are beyond renewal and reform. We need restructuring: a complete overhaul of the current system toward quality.

The critical incidents recorded during the interviews with principals can be classified according to quality. Of the 339 total incidents, 125 are related to quality in some way. An analysis of those incidents shows two separate categories of quality: quality of product and quality of experience. The fact that a quality school is defined by both product and experience was a common theme when principals were asked to describe a quality school:

> In a quality school, you would feel an enthusiasm to be there—staff and kids. I think of a school with multiple activities going on and, as our funding goes down, that is a piece of quality that will be lost. Because I do think if you are going to be equitable to all of the kids you need many programs. I think a quality school does meet the benchmark standards that are there and at least works toward them. I think a quality school is one that not only the kids are learning, but the teachers have opportunity for learning as well.—*medium-sized rural high school*

> I see a quality school as one in which the students are educated academically and socially, and the physical plant is safe, attractive, and it works not just on the academic side, but works for the whole child as well. The quality school has enough staff development to keep teachers working toward best practices.—*large suburban middle school*

> There should be a happy marriage between qualitative and quantitative measures. State of the art. It depends on what you compare it to. It should be useful and practical. The ability to make a silk purse out of a sow's ear—in other words, to take what you have been given and make the most out of it, measured qualitatively and quantitatively.—*large, urban high school*

Quality of Product

Quality of product refers to anything that can be easily quantified by a number. In my data, 35 percent (44 of the 125) of the quality critical incidents can be classified as quality of product. Anything that can be easily measured and compared across schools is a quality-of-product incident. Examples include test-score achievement, test-score improvement, attendance rates, dropout percentage, number of students going on to education beyond high school, percent of students achieving a diploma, volunteer hours in the school, number of teachers with master's degrees or years of teaching experience, and number of suspensions and expulsions. All of these things and many more can be easily measured and compared across schools. I have defined all of these "hard data" as quality of product: easily measured and easily compared. Because these data are easily measured and compared, they are used to create state and national report cards.

Quality of Experience

Quality of experience refers to data gathered through interviews, surveys, or observations. I have termed this kind of information "soft data" because it is more difficult to measure and more difficult to compare across schools. It takes a greater time investment.

When principals talk about the clubs in their school, surveying students to find out their interests, sports programs, parent and community attitudes, providing intramurals, having a great school climate, enrichment opportunities, community service, or mentor programs, these incidents are all quality of experience. When principals talk about quality, 65 percent of the time the things they mention are in the quality of experience domain.

One principal captured the essence of both quality of product and quality of experience in the following statement:

> A quality school is student centered. It looks at the needs of the students first and actually listens to the students and lets them provide input into the decision-making. They allow the parents and the staff input into the decision-making. A quality school has goals. Those goals are analyzed and reviewed on a yearly basis. When they form those goals, the school improvement plan actually becomes the living/working document for that school year. They are truly focused on improving—making the students a product of excellence and one where the school uses the resources in an equitable and effective manner. Resources are provided as much as possible on an as-needed basis. If we don't have those resources available, we find ways to do it either by fundraising or business partnerships, or writing grants—whatever it takes to meet the need.—*large urban middle school*

Although quality of product seems to be the most important element to the stakeholders of schools—the public at large, policymakers, and district personnel—quality of experience is the most important element to the primary customers of schools—the students and the parents who send their children into the building. For this reason, principals mention quality of experience indicators two-thirds of the time in their conversations about quality. Figure 6.4 represents how quality of product and experience applies to QSI framework. As illustrated by the arrow, there will be an increase in the levels of quality of product and experience as excellence is achieved through equity.

RESTRUCTURING TO QUALITY

To reach the commitment of restructuring toward quality, we cannot focus on policy demands, whether they come from the state, the federal government, or the district office. Focusing on policy will only result in renewal and reform. It is only by reaching beyond policy to the level of quality that we can restructure our schools.

Restructuring goes beyond what can be enforced through policy. Teachers in restructured schools describe the intrinsic rewards they derive from their increased success with students as the most powerful fac-

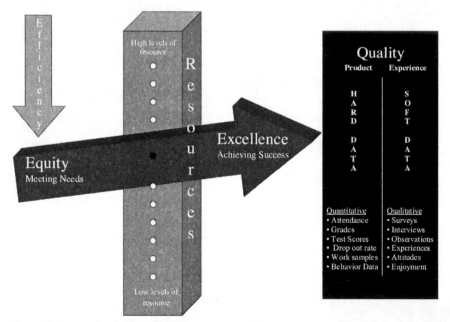

Figure 6.4. The Quality School Improvement Framework: Meeting needs (providing equity) will result in an increase of students achieving success (excellence), which will in turn increase the levels of quality (product and experience) for all constituents of the school.

tor that keeps them engaged in the difficult work of transforming their practice and changing their school (Darling-Hammond 1997). Research by Rosenholtz (1989) supports Darling-Hammond's claims by showing that the opportunity to be successful is the single most powerful motivator for entering and staying in the teaching profession.

The driving force in quality schools that raise the bar and bridge the achievement gap is the deep conviction held by all or most of the adults in the school that all students can be motivated to master essential skills and be successful. The importance of high staff expectations for student achievement and performance is well documented by the effective schools research (Edmonds 1979). Based on our experience in Lebanon, Oregon (see chapters 7 and 8), the highest level of quality improvement can only be achieved from within through restructuring, rather than from without via policies (reform).

Rowan (1990) distinguished between two types of organizational change strategies for bringing about improved student performance: control and commitment. Control strategies are external and imposed by government policies, the central office, or even the principal's office. Commitment strategies are intrinsically motivated, build capacity, and result in quality (Schmoker and Wilson 1993).

The No Child Left Behind Act is an extensive control strategy. If meeting its demands becomes the focus of districts or schools, they will never reach the level of commitment needed to restructure the school around quality. The quality schools of tomorrow have their sights set on things much more noble than this legislation, and I predict that in time these schools will leave the Act behind as they restructure themselves around the needs of students.

BREAKTHROUGH SCHOOLS

Schools around the nation are beginning to network to support school improvement efforts. Fullan (2003) maintains that regional and societal connections are mandatory for wholesale, effective change to occur— and practicing principals need to lead the way. A grassroots organization of schools has been formed to support and energize a revolution in school improvement.

A website, breakthroughschools.org, has been set up to lend support, encouragement, and help to any school willing to make a commitment to breakthrough results—defined as schools in which 90 percent of all learners are achieving benchmarks. As any principal knows, it takes a whole lot of effort to get that kind of result and continuous improvement to stay there. The purpose of breakthroughschools.org is to strengthen and encourage principals, teachers, and other school leaders to keep at it, and to share information and resources to make school improvement more efficient. Through the strength of networking, our schools can become better places to be. I encourage you to visit breakthroughschools.org and lend your hand to the continuous improvement of public schools in America.

Discussion Points

1. This chapter introduces the QSI (Quality School Improvement) framework. In what ways could this framework apply to school improvement in your district?
2. The QSI argues that the priority of meeting needs (equity) is the key to success and high levels of quality. Do you agree or disagree? Why or why not?
3. We can probably all agree that meeting student needs is the right thing to do. But the key to restructuring is making meeting needs *the* priority. What are the current priorities of your school or district, and how could your organization be restructured around student needs to a greater degree?
4. In what ways is your school or district measuring, monitoring, and achieving quality of product and quality of experience?

7

PRIORITY LEADERSHIP: HOW LEBANON SCHOOLS MANAGE THE TRIANGLE OF TENSION

We all need to choose to do a few things very, very, well. We've been asked to do about everything in the last ten years. We need to narrow the field, determine what the priorities are, and let everyone know— these are the priorities and then get out and get them done.—*large suburban high school*

An effective strategy for surviving the triangle of tension is by employing *priority leadership*. Priority leadership rejects goal setting. Goal setting is narrow and shortsighted. Setting goals limits vision to what you can become and achieve. Determining priorities and relentlessly pursuing them is different than goal setting. Priority-based leadership focuses on the vision, the mission of the organization, and doesn't stop moving forward. Priority leadership supports continuous improvement.

I have been an administrator in Lebanon, Oregon, for the past seven years. This chapter is our district's story of a revolutionary vision to reject both social promotion and retention in an effort to see that all children progress through school at their own appropriate rate and level of learning. It is a determined effort to meet the demands of excellence and equity within the confines of the pressure-filled environment of efficiency.

GENERATING TENSION IN LEBANON

Our story begins in the fall of 1999. Not a fan of the status quo, Lebanon Community School District's (LCSD) new superintendent, Jim Robinson, had spent some time measuring the climate for change. Now he was ready to move forward—even if the weather did seem a bit cold. When faced with wholesale, scary change, the most courageous way to implement it is to just do it and watch the chaos unfold. In public education that kind of leadership style might not result in guaranteed contracts, but it will generate change.

Jim's philosophy of change was not one of wading. By wading, he knew he would be hard pressed to get past his ankles before his tenure was up, and making it to his knees would take a Herculean effort. Going above the waist would be impossible . . . so he just charged right in.

Community forums were conducted, and the message from the community was clear: Something radical needed to be done about student achievement. Lebanon is a small rural town of 14,000 nestled in the heart of the Willamette Valley in Oregon. Halfway between Salem and Eugene, Lebanon is a logging community in transition. Like much of middle America, Lebanon has experienced its share of change during the downsizing of America. Mills have closed, unemployment has spiked, and poverty has increased. Most of Lebanon's eight schools have more than 50 percent of their students on free and reduced lunch. Since the inception of statewide testing comparisons, Lebanon students have never approached the state average. We have always been underachieving. That's who we were, and we had a lot of excuses for our underperformance, ranging from "it's the kids we have" to "it's the parents in our community that don't value education." Like many districts and schools, there was very little ownership in the educational community of our achievement problem.

Priority 1—The Student Achievement System (SAS): A Quest for Equity

From the beginning, Dr. Robinson was fond of saying that "average and ordinary are not acceptable." Lebanon schools would achieve, and he would find a way to make that possible. Community forums quickly surfaced the key issue. Students were progressing from grade to grade without the necessary academic skills. The end result was a high school full of students unprepared to be successful. They were on trajectories of failure that even the most elaborate high school recovery and alternative programs couldn't fix. Like many places across America, we were really good at social promotion, and rightly so—we'd been practicing it for a long time.

In spite of over two decades of daunting retention research that concludes students who are held back become prime targets for future failure, Jim jumped in. Something radical needed to be done. With encouragement from the school board, district leadership created the Student Achievement System (SAS), a systematic way of measuring student achievement that created yearly performance targets for students based on state tests and district performance assessments. Promotion standards were developed in reading, writing, math, and speaking. Students had to demonstrate mastery on state tests and district performance assessments before they would be promoted to the next grade level. They had to demonstrate what they knew and were able to do. With one big push, the pendulum was sent swinging away from social promotion and toward retention. As you can imagine, we were sent into an immediate disequilibrium.

Initially, teachers, students, and parents were in an uproar. We soon found out that talking about achievement and taking drastic steps to guarantee achievement were two very different things. Increasing student achievement was a great idea that looked nice on paper, but taking a bold step to bring it about through promotion standards was painful. That first year, 15 to 20 percent of our students were not able to meet the promotion standards and were afforded more time at their current grade level, and though some parents struggled with the new standards, we found teachers had difficulty with retention as well. It was crushing for them to share the bad news with parents that their child would be repeating a grade level.

Many parents, however, had a different response. They were pleased that we were taking a bold step toward guaranteeing achievement, and although retention was never preferred for a child, it was appreciated because many parents instinctively realized that moving their child forward without the necessary academic skills would only ensure failure at some future point.

In Michael Fullan's *Moral Imperative* (2003), he describes what is known as the "Implementation Dip." The dip illustrates the fact that when systematic change is implemented, there is usually an initial drop in performance before improvement can be seen. This is because people in the system have to adjust to the change and learn new skills in the process. Our 15-percent failure rate and the stress of that first year of SAS implementation was indicative of that dip, and when we realized that retention wasn't the solution either, we started to pull out of it.

Efficiency Takes Its Toll: No New Money After our second year of implementation, the system didn't feel right. Yes, we had effectively halted social promotion. Students were not moving to the next grade level without the skills they needed to be successful. However, we had replaced social promotion with retention: Students who failed the first time around were getting similar treatment the second time, and in many cases, the extra year didn't result in an increase in learning because we were not meeting their needs. Students were not getting additional or different interventions, and we all pointed our finger at Salem, the major source of our operating budget. We needed more money to do it right.

Most of the retention programs implemented around the country involve extra money that buys additional summer school sessions and instruction for those who do not meet standards. The resources are marshaled so that students who are lacking can "catch up." The approach in Lebanon took a different turn.

We didn't have any new money. We couldn't even find money to keep our regular programs operating. Our funding was flat throughout the initial implementation period, and in the spring of 2003, we experienced a statewide budget crisis that was the worst in our district's history. As a result, we were forced to cut our overall budget by 10 percent, which resulted in a teacher reduction of forty positions. It was hardly an environment to foster innovation, but through the financial struggle, new thinking emerged.

Meeting Student Needs Becomes the Focus: A Reflection of Equity The unintended consequences of our retention program began to surface. Students who were retained were losing motivation and feeling defeated. They missed the mark for promotion and were now sent around the carousel again. Holding students back a year was in many cases a demotivator, and the only thing worse for a teacher than an underskilled student is an *unmotivated*, underskilled student. Through hard work, effective instruction, and a great deal of effort, students with low skills can achieve over time, but the unmotivated and underskilled just get further and further behind. Our experience, coupled with the body of research regarding retention, convinced us that retention was not the solution.

It was during this time that the SAS moved to the next level. Rejecting social promotion and avoiding retention requires a restructuring of the educational system around the resource of time, and this can only happen when a new paradigm is conceived regarding equity that is relentlessly pursued to meet the needs of the individual student.

It became clear that we would not be able to meet student needs without taking on the adaptive challenge of finding the balance between social promotion and retention. In its current form, the SAS rejects both social promotion and retention, with social promotion defined as sending students on to the next grade level unprepared academically, and retention defined as doing the same thing for two years in a row. What has emerged in our schools can now be seen as the beginning stages of a continuous progress model.

Lebanon's Continuous Progress Model of Instruction   In Lebanon schools, students advance to the next level of learning when they are ready. The result has been remarkable. Grouping our schools by benchmarks rather than grades has created natural teams of teachers who work with groups of students with similar abilities. Students move through the benchmarks according to their learning and performance. Some students are able to move considerably faster, while others get the benefit of more time. The question shifted from, "Did they meet the standard?" to "What are we going to do differently so that they can meet the standard whenever they are ready?" We've also stumbled onto a new paradigm that occurs more frequently, "Now that they've met the standard ahead of schedule, what are we going to do so that their learning is not slowed down?"

Learning, like the development of the human body, is not static. Not everyone makes one year's growth in a year's time, and that shouldn't be the expectation. Some students can make two years or a year and a half's worth of progress in a year, and some students, because of absences or other life crises, might only make a half-year's growth. In our ungraded schools and multiage classrooms, students move seamlessly from one level to the next, all in cooperation and communication with parents. We have shifted our spotlight from impartial standards to student need, and since student need is the focus, there are no limits to what students can achieve. The result of pursuing the purest form of equity—meeting each student's need—has been liberating. In this way, every student is not only motivated but successful as well.

Because the fundamental philosophy behind the SAS is meeting student needs, we no longer make excuses about our lack of resources. Once needs are discovered, efficiencies can usually be found within the system to address them. It is amazing how creative and resourceful a group of educators can be when faced with the dilemma of meeting a student's need.

In connection with parents, students who are not academically ready to be successful at the next benchmark level of instruction are provided more time and different instruction at their current level of performance until they demonstrate mastery. In this way, every child is successful. Seamless entry and exit through the grade levels and benchmarks when students are ready has moved us beyond the notion of "June only" promotions. In our continuous progress model, students can move through classrooms and benchmarks whenever they are ready.

When a student is not making adequate progress, a team of teachers meets to determine what the student needs, and then we creatively marshal our resources to meet that need. We have also discovered that when a parent knows our top priority is meeting the need of their child, obtaining their cooperation and support is surprisingly easy. They are more than willing to partner for their child's success.

Breakthrough Results   In Lebanon, we are achieving excellence through the meeting of student needs. All of our schools have one common denominator, equity—meeting student needs in creative, cost-saving ways and providing instruction at the rate and pace that will be most effective—and the results are starting to show. Figures 7.1 and 7.2 shows the test scores in reading for all eight of our schools over a six-year period. Our improvement efforts have resulted in not only approaching the state averages in achievement but surpassing them as well. We started below the norm and have achieved to beyond the norm. In reading (figure 7.1), our students went from meeting state standards

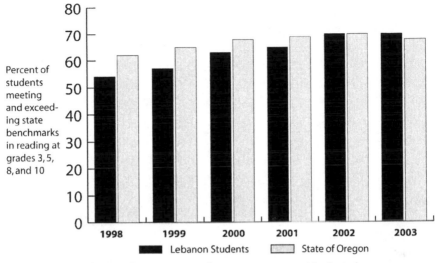

Figure 7.1. LCSD reading test score improvement over the last six years.

at a rate of 52 percent to 70 percent over a six-year period. In mathematics (figure 7.2), the improvement gains are still significant, but not as sharp (from 48 to 62 percent) because our instructional practices in mathematics haven't undergone as much restructuring. We started with reading. Math is our next target.

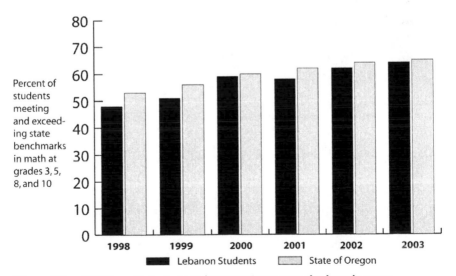

Figure 7.2. LCSD math test score improvement over the last six years.

The improvement we have experienced is not in just a few schools. The charts represent students tested at grades 3, 5, 8, and 10 in all of our schools over six years. Although improvement is a complex study, we can't help but think the raising of expectations via the SAS—and the improvement of teaching techniques as teachers discovered new ways to meet student needs—has had a dramatic effect over the last six years. The SAS system has improved instruction, which has resulted in levels of sustained improvement that are seldom reached in school reform in spite of the increased pressures of accountability legislation.

The shift to a continuous progress model has been messy and often confusing. We are still in what Jim Collins (2001) refers to as the period of build-up. Our goal of breakthrough achievement will be realized when we consistently see 90 percent of our students achieving state standards up through the high school level. We are currently hitting that average in most of our schools at grades 3 and 5, but still have some ground to gain at grades 8 and 10.

Priority 2—Signature Schools: A Quest for Excellence

We have come to realize that breakthrough results will not be possible without innovation, and to facilitate innovation, our superintendent introduced the concept of *signature schools.* Dr. Robinson realized early on that to achieve the adaptive challenges necessary to develop a continuous progress model, he would need to give each school the autonomy to act. Only through such autonomy would restructuring be possible. In chapter 8, I discuss the signature innovations implemented at Pioneer School that enabled us to balance equity (meeting student needs) with the pursuit of excellence (achievement) during a time of flat funding and budget reduction (efficiency).

Signature schools by definition are high achieving, invitational, and innovative schools. The expectation is achievement, the culture is invitational, and the means to achieve both is through innovation. In LCSD, schools are encouraged to innovate. The result has been a fertile ground for experimental calendars, after-school programs, schools-within-a-school, and special schedules. This year, the eight schools in Lebanon operate on four different calendars. Time has been reorganized through creative intersessions in which portions of the student body return to school for intensive small-group instruction. Some of the sessions focus on helping students who have not yet met standards and can greatly benefit from targeted, small-group instruction. Other sessions focus on enrichment activities that expand the curriculum for students who have exceeded the standards.

Lebanon High School received a substantial grant from the federal government to restructure into smaller learning communities and also received a million-dollar grant from the Bill and Melinda Gates Foundation for their innovative restructuring efforts.

After-school programs have been developed in our elementary schools, in which instructional aides trained in reading and math instruction lead groups of children in remedial efforts, and split dismissal schedules, in which teachers work with small groups of children from their own classroom who have not yet met standards.

Lebanon also instituted districtwide a behavior-modification program known as *PBS (Positive Behavior Support)* that follows the implementation plan presented in the recently published *BEST Training Manual* (Sprague and Golly 2003). This program has fostered invitational environments throughout our schools. It is a systemic plan to teach (and reteach) expected student behaviors, recognize (and reward) those who are demonstrating the expected behaviors, and enforce consistent consequences when the universal behaviors are not followed. Through this districtwide approach, our schools have seen dramatic improvements in student behavior. Across the district, student referrals have been reduced by 50 percent. Such an improvement in behavior and the stellar implementation of this model has made our district a national and international demonstration site for PBS. During the 2003–2004 school year alone, we entertained teams of educators from the Netherlands, Norway, and several states across the country to see PBS in action. Without question, making our schools safer and more invitational has had a direct impact on student learning and time on task.

Priority 3—Effective Instruction: Professional Growth and Accountability (PGA) System

Elmore and Burney (1999) make it clear that the most important element for school improvement is an investment in instruction. The authors maintain that, "it is about instruction and only instruction, and that instruction change is a long, multistage process" (1999, 266). In Lebanon, we agree. Realizing the importance of instruction, we have developed a system of standards that define quality instruction. Our Professional Growth & Accountability (PGA) System (Lebanon Supervision and Evaluation Task Force 2001) combines the notion of both intrinsic growth and extrinsic accountability to the profession of teaching.

The development of the system began in the fall of 1997, using the work of Charlotte Danielson (1996) as a framework. Over a three-year period, a team of administrators, teachers, and outside specialists developed a comprehensive system that describes what excellent instruction looks like, sounds like, and feels like. Although it is true that defining quality teaching doesn't guarantee great instruction, the manual has given administrators and teachers alike targets to aim for in their quest for continuous improvement.

We have recently discovered a technology tool through eCOVE.net that brings the power of computing to classroom observations for the first time. The eCOVE software has dozens of teacher and student tools to facilitate data-driven observation of student and teacher behavior in the classroom. Developed by an educator at Willamette University (Tenny 2004) over the course of twenty years, the software links research about teaching and learning to every tool. We plan to use this tool to further improve our PGA system to help teachers continually perfect their craft.

In our system a variety of instruction-embedded performance assessments and observations help teams of teachers constantly assess what a student needs to maximize learning. In this way, students who are not being successful are quickly identified and provided with the resources they need.

CONCLUSION

The SAS system in Lebanon is an ongoing, grassroots effort. We didn't read about it in a book somewhere. It was birthed through painful innovation—which began with a rejection of the status quo. There is no prescribed path to quality, and there are no easy answers to resolving the triangle of tension. However, we have discovered that improvement toward high levels of quality begins with setting priorities and sticking to them. We have also learned that achieving high levels of quality is different for every school because every school has different professionals with different strengths and weaknesses, hence the importance of signature schools. The final priority in the Lebanon example is quality instruction. Systems must be developed that improve instructional quality, the most important element of school improvement.

Discussion Points

1. What priorities does your school or district have? Can you name them easily? Have those priorities been stable over a period of years?
2. What priorities should your district or school develop? What is important to your students? Parents? Community members? Staff? District office? What is important to you?
3. If you were to determine priority number one, what would it be, and how would you implement it?

8

APPLYING THE QSI IN THE SCHOOL SETTING

Wanted: A miracle worker who can do more with less, pacify rival groups, endure chronic second-guessing, tolerate low levels of support, process large volumes of paper and work double shifts (75 nights a year). He or she will have carte blanche to innovate, but cannot spend much money, replace any personnel, or upset any constituency.—Robert Evans (1995)

The school principal at the local level faces the most pressure from the triangle of tension. As revealed in the interviews I conducted, the pressures of striving to achieve excellence, equity, and efficiency can be overwhelming. Michael Fullan states: "It is likely that only a minority of school principals are even working at the 25 percent level of depth of moral purpose . . . a depth that improves, for example, reading scores of students" (2003, 41).

The mandate to improve through innovation is both liberating and frightening. It is liberating to have license to experiment, look for new solutions, and create programs that will generate improvement and result in student learning. It is downright scary at times to realize that the status quo is not acceptable, that change is expected and even required.

PIONEER SCHOOL—MY STORY

I am the principal of Pioneer School in Lebanon, Oregon. Pioneer is a K–8 school of 500 students located on the border of the city of Lebanon and the surrounding countryside. We have a high population of free and reduced students—just over 70 percent in March 2004. We have the highest percentage of disabled students in the district. At last count, 15 percent of our students had an Individualized Education Plan (IEP) of some kind. We also have the highest percentage of students in transition. Last year, more than 107 of our students left at some time during the school year, and 100 enrolled after the year started. The high mobility rate means that about 20 percent of the faces in June weren't there in September. Educators talk about the difficulties of teaching the disabled, minorities, the poor, or ESL students. But none of those groups presents the challenges of the absent—those who simply aren't in schools all year, either because of a high absentee rate or moving from place to place.

Pioneer School is new. We just completed our second full year of operation. In the spring of 2000, the Lebanon community passed a bond to build two new schools, upgrade others, and close ones in decay. The bond passage was a landmark achievement for our community. It was the first time in more than fifty years that a bond had been passed in Lebanon.

Puzzle Building

In the spring of 2004, I was asked by the district curriculum committee to review the progress of my school toward achieving the goal of continuous progress, and they wanted my answer in the metaphor of a puzzle. After two schools and five years of Student Achievement System (SAS) implementation in Lebanon, I really had to think about it. Without a doubt I was working hard—really hard. My days were full and busy, but what did I have to show for it, and could I describe my progress toward the vision of continuous progress in terms of a puzzle? How far along was I in the design? What percentage of the puzzle was completed?

At first I balked at the request. I wasn't building a puzzle, and I couldn't define what was happening in my school in such concrete terms.

I didn't like the metaphor. I thought the process at Pioneer was more like a journey, a trip with an unknown destination, and I was just taking one turn after another trying to keep the car on the road as it continued to gain speed and momentum. I went home and thought about it. Unfortunately, my work was more like driving a car to an unknown destination than the building of a deliberate puzzle, and that began to bother me.

So much of the work of a principal is spent putting out fires, moving from one crisis to the next with barely room to breathe, let alone eat lunch, respond to the blinking voice mail, open up the pile of e-mail or, heaven forbid, be the instructional leader of a school. The truly important work generally takes second place to the urgent. At least that is the ongoing temptation and nature of the pull in schools. The good is the enemy of the best. And because so much of the day demands our management, we are never quite able to get to the leadership part. I realized that not making time for leadership was one of the most frustrating aspects of being a principal. I *was* just trying to steer a car racing downhill without brakes, and I should have been building a puzzle. Steering cars is management. Building puzzles is leadership.

Puzzles are complex. They take time and thought to build. There are no right ways to build a puzzle, but there are some guidelines that can help. For starters, it helps to have the box top to look at. What is the ultimate vision? What is the end in mind? What kind of system was I trying to construct? For me, the answer to that question was easy, and it was an opportunity to apply the Quality School Improvement framework to my own organization.

According to the QSI, the entire success of the system hinges on meeting student needs—ensuring equity as defined by equal opportunity to the fullest extent possible. My theory was simple: When the needs of the individual are met, the collective will achieve success. Now I had an opportunity to prove it. The Pioneer puzzle would be complete when I could meet those needs in creative, cost-efficient ways. Building puzzles begins with borders, and the first thing to do is find the corners. What were my big ideas? What was the foundation of my vision of meeting needs?

I have always believed in the power of relationships, not just positive relationships between teachers and students and parents, but meaningful relationships between teachers as well. Educators have always placed a great emphasis on relationships. Roland Barth boldly asserts: "I learned over and over again that the relationship among the adults in the schoolhouse has more impact on the quality and the character of the school—and on the accomplishment of youngsters—than any other factor" (2001, 105).

Bottom Border: Relationships   It became clear that the bottom border of my puzzle must be relationships. To facilitate the power of relationships and teacher efficacy, we divided our K–8 school of 500 students into smaller schools-within-a-school and turned off the bells. It was the single best decision we ever made. Bells no longer ruled our school, and that simple innovation gave teachers autonomy over their own environment. Teachers, our leading learners, were now directing the charge. Because the state standards are divided into benchmarks of learning, we divided our teams according to the benchmark distinctions. Benchmark I encompassed grades K–3, benchmark II grades 4–5, and benchmark III grades 6–8.

Through trial and error, we discovered that teacher teams of more than five are considerably less effective when it comes to meeting student needs. The ideal number for close-working teams of teachers is three to five. Fewer than three doesn't provide enough diversity of ideas, and more than five diminishes the power of teacher teams because it becomes too time-consuming and complex to organize, meet, share ideas, and problem solve together. The most effective teacher teams are those that self-organize and are run by teachers. That doesn't happen when the numbers get too big. It is through the power of efficacy that teacher teams become most effective. There must be intrinsic motivation, ownership, and buy-in for teacher teams to be successful.

At Pioneer, we ended up with four teams: five teachers at benchmark I, four at benchmark II, three at benchmark IIIA, and four at benchmark IIIB. It has been amazing to see the level of buy-in and commitment these teams have developed. They share curriculum, ideas for instruction, students, and strategies to reach students who are falling behind. We truly experienced what we knew intuitively all the time: that the collective is smarter for solving problems than the individual. When it comes to teaming, the whole is greater than the sum of its parts.

Relationships are central. Achievement gaps are bridged by the power of relationships. Research is clear that students of color as well as those from backgrounds of poverty will learn more if they have a positive relationship with their teacher (Cooper 2004). Teacher teams build relationships by supporting one another when they have difficult children. As they meet on a regular basis to discuss student needs, they are able to obtain help from their colleagues in designing structures to meet those needs.

Instruction: Time and How You Use It

In education, student achievement is the direct result of improved instruction. Elmore and Burney (1999), among many others, have documented that the quality of instruction is the single most important factor when it comes to improving student learning. Highly skilled teachers are constantly reflecting upon their own work to see how it can be improved. Change is a necessary ingredient for improvement.

Change is intentional and complex. In *From Good to Great* (2001), Jim Collins documents companies all over the United States that made the jump from being good to being great. According to Collins, the number one element in successful change is determining what you will never change—your priorities—and once those are determined, you have the chance to move from good to great. Going from good to great requires a series of efforts, and in schools, improving the quality of instruction students receive must be the ongoing, ever-present priority.

Collins likens improvement to the metaphor of turning a huge, heavy flywheel. You push and push and push to achieve one turn, and then another, and then another. This is the period of buildup. Momentum is built by focusing on working through your priorities, and over time the flywheel begins to turn faster and faster. Then comes the period of breakthrough, when greatness is achieved. Most school improvement efforts are not sustained because somewhere along the way, intention is lost. Perhaps there is a change in leadership. The average school superintendent doesn't stay in a district longer than three years. Breakthrough results cannot be achieved in such a short time. Sometimes intention is lost because the work becomes too difficult. Having priorities sustains you through the difficult period of buildup.

Instruction can be defined in terms of time, with the twofold goal of both improving the instructional quality and increasing the amount of instructional time provided for students. The use of time is an untapped resource in schools across the United States. Like our brains and the computers on the desks, we use far less than our potential. The next breakthrough in public education will occur as we discover not only how to create more time for student learning, but even more important, how to use that time more effectively.

In recent years, the quality revolution has brought data to our doorsteps, but for the most part, educators haven't opened that door. There is simply too much to do. Just the other day, I had a principal tell me that he "just wasn't a data guy." However, when it comes to using data effectively, principals must lead the charge or the innovations will not spread to the classroom. We will never learn how to tap the resource of time until we become proficient at using the data already at our fingertips. Through the proper and consistent use of data, teachers can learn how to use their class time more effectively. We have been inundated with data in recent years, but the data provided are not made available to teachers in ways they can easily access to make instructional decisions for kids. The next level of school improvement will be reached when administrators and teachers learn how to use technology to effectively access the massive power hidden in the mines of data all around us.

Unlocking the door of data to drive instructional decisions is an adaptive challenge. Ron Heifetz (2004) defines an adaptive challenge as problems with solutions that cannot be easily or readily solved. In other words, there are two kinds of problems: those you have the knowledge and resources to solve and those you do not.

We have the knowledge and resources to solve technical problems. Management is all about technical problems: taking care of business; getting done what we know how to do, and doing it in a timely manner. For most principals, the school day is filled with one tedious management task after another. Good managers get it all done and keep people happy in the process. For most public schools in the United States, good management is more than enough to get an extended contract and keep you out of the superintendent's hot seat.

Adaptive challenges are those problems that are beyond our knowledge and resource base. When it comes to improvement, most of the problems we face are adaptive challenges. Adaptive challenges are complex because the solution cannot be easily discerned. Leadership is all about adaptive challenges. Most principals don't have or make much time to tackle adaptive challenges. As a result, there is little overall sustained improvement in schools. Priority leadership means having the courage and fortitude to take on one adaptive challenge after another.

There are many creative ways to increase instructional time that are cost efficient, and although we at Pioneer School certainly weren't the creators of any of these innovations, they each proved to be an adaptive challenge for our school that we pursued for the sole purpose of increasing instructional time without an increase of resources. At Pioneer, innovations regarding the reorganization of time became the top, left, and right borders of our school-improvement puzzle.

Pushing the Borders of Time

Pioneer School was completed in the fall of 2002 as the last of three K–8 schools in Lebanon. The students of Pioneer and our staff came together from four surrounding smaller schools that were all closed. The staff was not hand picked by the district office or myself. Prior to the reconstituting of our district, each principal developed a *signature*, or vision, of what he or she hoped to pursue. Teachers interested in the published vision elected to go to that particular school.

Because we were new, we had the advantage of creating a new culture, and the culture we created was based on determining ways to meet student needs. The diverse staff brought lots of new ideas and energy. Learning how to coordinate that energy and determine a direction was an adaptive challenge that required leadership, and the first smart thing I did was recognize and teach that everyone could and *should* lead. This wasn't a unique idea:

> The more educators are a part of the decision-making, the greater their morale, participation, and commitment in carrying out the goals of the school. Imagine a school where *every* teacher takes ownership for a portion of the organization! When many lead, the school wins. (Barth 2001, 82)

As we tackled our adaptive challenges via shared leadership, we soon discovered that brilliant ideas and solutions came from all quarters of our

organization. The result was a reorganization of time that manifested itself in three programs—an after-school program, a summer school, and
an intersession calendar—which were all implemented within a three-
year time frame. These innovations occurred during a season of unprecedented budget reduction across the district and state.

After-School Program   The left border of the Pioneer puzzle is our
after-school program. In our school of 500 students, more than 130 are
involved in the program. We have three sessions throughout the year
that run from 2:15 to 3:00 PM. At parent conferences, teachers identify
the students who can benefit the most from intensive, small-group instruction and invite them to participate in these sessions. As a result,
students who need more time to learn can receive it—over 100 hours of
it every year. This instruction is premium, small-group teaching that targets exactly what the students need to be successful.

The curriculum and materials for the classes are developed by our Title I and special-education teachers, who work together determining
what students need to learn each session. Seven-hour instructional
aides, who work until 3:00 PM, deliver the instruction in small groups.
Not only do the students' skills increase, but the instructional aides become more effective instructors as well. This provides teachers throughout the school with a common planning time that is necessary for effective teaming to occur.

Our after-school program is able to meet needs on several levels. Not
only does it provide quality, small-group instruction for the most needy
students in our system, but it also provides time for teachers to plan, assess, and collaborate with colleagues. During our state-assessment win-
dow, some teachers even use this time to provide extra instruction to
needy students. The program also improves the teaching skills of our instructional aides, who work directly with the children in the small
groups. Such skill improvement not only helps the students during the
after-school program, but these skills are carried over into their regular
work throughout the school day.

Quality instruction is the number one factor in school improvement.
Quality instruction is more than time in front of students; it also requires
planning and assessment. The quality-improvement cycle of instruction
is planning, instruction, and assessment. Teachers need time by themselves and with teammates to effectively plan. Instruction occurs with

children; then comes assessment. The two kinds of assessment are: student assessment and instructional reflection. Over the last fifteen years we have learned a great deal about the importance of assessing students on what they can and cannot do. These performance assessments are a necessary component to student learning. Just as valuable are a teacher's self-assessments, which I call instructional reflectionwhen teachers reflect on their instruction, what they communicated, and how they can improve their teaching. Edward Deming (1986), the founder of the modern quality movement, believed strongly that self-corrections and meaningful reflection were of more value for improvement than any time-consuming, close observations by supervisors.

Summer School   The right border of our puzzle is a three-week, half-day summer school for the thirty-six most needy benchmark I students in our school. Funding for this can happen by creating a flexible work year for our Title I teacher and setting aside some of our school-wide Title I funds for a teacher stipend. Knowing that the research strongly supports the importance of children learning how to read before the fourth grade, we identify our thirty-six most needy students in grades 1–3 in May and invite them to a fifteen-session, half-day, small group instruction in August. We have found that our most needy students will gain far more from a three-week intensive session in August then they will from any whole group instruction. By purchasing some aide time as well, the summer school sessions end up having a ratio of one adult for every six students—an ideal balance for effective small-group instruction.

Intersession Calendar   The intersession calendar, pioneered by another school in our district, frames the top of our puzzle. We shifted to an intersession calendar because of the flexibility it created to meet student needs. Students in our district receive 176 days of instruction. The comparatively large number of days enables us to easily meet the state minimum of time for each grade level. On the intersession calendar, all students receive 172 days of regular instruction. Students also have the opportunity to attend an intersession designed to meet their needs. We divided the staff into thirds and provide intersessions at three times during the year. One is a week before school starts, one is the week after spring break, and one is the week after school gets out in June.

Each intersession has a different purpose. The August intersession focuses on students who need more time to meet benchmarks and is designed to help them get a jump start on the school year. At Pioneer, our students take their state tests on the computer throughout the school year when they are ready. This enables us to have real-time feedback and assessment of their performance. In this way, we are able to focus the March intersession on the students who have not yet met the state benchmark level. Through small-group, intensive instruction, they are provided more time to focus on the areas needing growth. Our June intersession is designed for our students who need an extra challenge. This challenge comes in many forms, including experiential learning, hands-on activities, and problem-solving scenarios that cannot be done with large groups. We also work with students who do not yet have the required work samples to be promoted to the next benchmark during the June intersession and need additional small-group instruction. Often, the only thing a student needs is one sample in one area, and often extra practice, instruction, and time is all they need to make it. Through our intersession calendar, we can provide that time.

More Pieces to the Puzzle

School improvement is complex. It is also intentional. Positive change can happen over time if a group of people are willing to take on leadership roles, use each other as a resource to solve problems, and keep working at it. It takes a commitment that will not waiver. The foundation of our improvement effort is relationships. In our effort to meet student needs, we have pushed the borders of time to create three innovative systemic changes that did not need additional funding from outside sources to start or maintain. These three programs have created a potential of almost 300 hours of additional instruction for any student who might need it. Because a school year consists of approximately 900 hours of instruction, we've created an additional third of a school year without incurring any additional costs.

However, we all know that learning is more than just time. It is also how you use that time. All of the interior pieces of our puzzle are a function of how we use time. The next wave of school improvement will focus on how time is used—using it more effectively and getting the most out of every minute provided. The following list shows the interior of our puzzle. They are examples of some of the ways we use time effectively to affect student learning.

- **Assessment of all new students:** Before any new student is placed in a classroom, assessments are conducted in reading, writing, and math so that, we know the student's academic level and can make a match with the classroom most suited to his or her learning needs.
- **Positive behavior support (PBS):** This systematic, schoolwide behavior-modification program has reduced our office referrals by more than 50 percent. We have come to realize that students will learn much more in positive, safe environments. PBS, a research-based program developed at the University of Oregon (Sprague and Golly 2003), creates that kind of positive environment. The program focuses on three elements: teaching (and reteaching) expected behavior, reinforcing that behavior through a system of meaningful rewards, and providing logical consequences when the expected behaviors are not followed. Supporting our PBS system, we have a problem-solving room that is devoted to meeting both the academic and behavioral needs of students throughout the day. We have found this kind of support to be crucial in making our system work effectively.
- **Service learning:** All of our classrooms are involved in some kind of service learning project during the school year. Some classes are involved in several. We believe in the hands-on, minds-on approach to learning. When students are involved in real-world problems, their interest level and engagement in learning increase. It gives them a break from the monotony of regular school. We have never and will never let the pressure of high-stakes testing keep us from having a strong service-learning component in our school. As a matter of fact, we believe that students who are regularly engaged in service learning projects will do *better* on standardized assessments because they will enjoy school more on every level.
- **Continuous progress report card:** We have designed a K–12 schoolwide report card that represents visually what a student has achieved and what he or she needs to achieve to meet the required standards. With such a report card, learning becomes the constant,

and time is the variable. Students are able to progress to the next level when they are ready, and they are no longer bound by yearly entry points. As a result, many of our students are progressing more rapidly through our benchmarks, and those—by far the minority—who need more time are able to get that time without the stigma of having failed. The report card also has a commitment to learning section that communicates to parents ways their child can improve in their commitment to learning at school.

- **Extensive community volunteer program:** We have actively marketed for and obtained the help of a wide range of volunteers. In addition to parents, we have foster grandparents, high school cadet teachers, and university students, and a local church has adopted us and sends volunteers our way to help throughout the school day. All of this extra help translates into hours upon hours of higher-quality, small-group instruction for kids. During the 2003–2004 school year, we logged more 5,600 hours of volunteer labor at our school.

- **Peer mentors:** Students are trained to help other students problem solve and look for solutions to the multitude of concerns they have. This kind of service learning project trains students how to resolve their own conflicts. Many times the resolutions are more effective than when the adults get involved.

- **Peer helpers:** In this program, older elementary students are trained to assist younger ones on the playground. They serve as friends when students are down and help adults become aware of playground squabbles.

- **Classroom mentors:** Because we are a K–8 school, we have created many opportunities for older students to work in classrooms with younger students as helpers and mentors. Again, this program—like all the others—is based on student need. Often, students will flourish when they have an opportunity to be the helper in another classroom. In one of our fourth-grade classes, the only thing that motivated one struggling girl was the opportunity to help in a second-grade classroom for the last thirty minutes of the day if she completed all her work with a good attitude. The turnaround in this girl's demeanor and work production in her classroom was astounding. This kind of mentor program helps not only the students receiving services, but even more so the student providing them by taking on a leadership role to meet someone else's need.

- **Online assessment:** Every school needs to reduce the impact of high-stakes testing and assessments. We have done that by migrating our entire testing program to the Oregon online version of TESA (Technology Enhanced System of Assessment). TESA not only levels questions to a student's ability, it also provides immediate feedback for the teacher and student so that instruction can be adjusted. It provides multiple opportunities for testing and increased flexibility for testing in general. At Pioneer, we no longer have the two power weeks when the whole school is testing. Our assessment is ongoing throughout the year. Students are always being assessed and their instruction being adjusted as a result—and it all is done according to student need. The online assessment system enables us to test our learning disabled students with accommodations that help us to determine what they actually know and are able to do instead of having them shut down because of the frustration of a paper-and-pencil test.

- **Accelerated math, reading, and writing:** A technology-based supplemental math, reading, and writing programs via Renaissance Learning can effectively provide differentiated instruction for all students in all grades. These programs are such powerful motivators for learning that students request them for free time. Students are able to learn math at their own level and receive immediate feedback and instruction. They read books and have their comprehension checked electronically, and they learn how to recognize outstanding writing and use that knowledge to improve their own writing through peer and teacher review.

- **Small Group Instruction:** I believe in the power of children working and learning together in small groups. At Pioneer, we make that kind of learning a priority. Whether it is our 8th graders working in teams in the technology lab to testing the aerodynamics of a car they designed or our 1st graders reading in a small group with an instructional assistant, we have put a high value on effective instructional groupings. We are not just talking about cooperative learning, where children are taught how to learn together and with each other, we are talking about trained professionals and volunteers working with and instructing small groups of children and one-on-one when necessary. At Pioneer, small-group instruction is a bedrock priority.

- **Teacher teams:** I cannot emphasize enough the importance and power of close-knit teams of teachers working together to meet student needs. Not only will effective teacher teams share curriculum and resources, but they will travel to conferences and learn together, challenge each other, and brainstorm ways to reach students. Teaching is a tough profession. Teachers spend the majority of their work day interacting with and directing the learning of curious children. This is taxing work. When teachers enjoy their teammates and work together well, the heavy load lightens a bit, new energies are discovered, and the children benefit in the end.

CONCLUSION

The programmatic items in this chapter are not comprehensive, but rather are shown to provide a sampling of how we use time at Pioneer to increase and maximize student learning. It is my belief that any school can achieve breakthrough results, in which 90 percent of the students meet or exceed state standards. Within two years of opening, Pioneer School—a school with the highest poverty ratio, the highest mobility rate in the district, and the highest percentage of learning disabled students—exceeded 90 percent of all our students (in grades 2–8) meeting and exceeding the state benchmarks in reading and math. Two years ago, I wouldn't have thought that was possible, but we have found that relentlessly focusing on meeting the needs of individual students is the key to surviving the triangle of tension—and achieving excellence.

Discussion Points

1. School improvement is complex. There are no cookie-cutter solutions, but it starts with determining student needs and then meeting those needs. Does the information from this chapter provide any creative ideas for how you might meet student needs in your school?
2. School improvement is also intentional. It begins with priorities and is sustained by sticking to those priorities. How much of your

principalship is governed by management tasks? How much is governed by leadership pursuits? What is the appropriate balance of each?

3. Quality instruction is central to school improvement. Quality instruction is based on time and how you use it. In what ways is your school using time effectively? In what ways is time being wasted or not used to its fullest potential? Are there certain instructional methods or tools that help teachers adjust their instruction to the needs of their learners that you are using or could benefit from using? How can the use of technology in the classroom aide in the effort to more effectively meet student needs?

9

PRINCIPALS: RECOMMENDATIONS FOR RESTRUCTURING

Because change is intentional (Collins 2001) and complex (Fullan 2004), it begins with courage and continues with commitment. It never ends. Moving a school down the road of restructuring begins with principals making a decision to do so. Fullan speaks of this commitment as "the moral imperative for principals" (2003, 41) and maintains that the principal must be the one involved in leading a deep culture change that mobilizes students, teachers, and parents to improve learning for all students. Collins's (2001) research revealed that disciplined, self-motivated people who don't need to be motivated are the key ingredient for an organization to make significant improvement. That being the case, the following recommendations for principals—if diligently applied—will push a school toward restructuring around student needs.

These recommendations are based in the body of effective schools research, quality school research, a synthesis of the data gleaned from conversations with principals, and my own ideas. The list is by no means exhaustive, but it does provide an excellent starting place for school improvement.

1. Invest in quality teachers.
2. Stress *client* service throughout the school.

3. Provide priority leadership: Determine a vision, build it, and communicate it effectively.
4. Build leadership capacity and teaming.
5. Emphasize continuous improvement in all areas by focusing on
   data-driven decision making and results.
6. Move away from "boss management" to "lead management."
7. Work with the central office.
8. Build a sense of community and create smallness.
9. Build and use networks.
10. Use tension generated from external demands as impetus for
    growth.
11. Instill hope and make it fun

INVEST IN QUALITY TEACHERS

The most crucial investment a principal can make is in well-qualified,
caring, and committed teachers. Without good teachers, even the best
reform initiatives cannot be implemented to their full potential (Riley
1998). Excellent teachers employ inquiry-oriented techniques, use
strategies that engage students in high levels of thinking, and individu-
alize their approaches through assessment and adaptation of the curriculum based on student need (Van Tassel-Baska 1997). When it comes
to meeting the needs of equity to achieve excellence, principals mentioned again and again the importance of teachers being able to differentiate instruction. High-quality teachers can and do differentiate instruction. McEwan's *Ten Traits of Highly Effective Teachers* (2002) is an
extremely valuable resource not only for identifying outstanding teachers but for helping develop quality teachers as well.

STRESS CLIENT SERVICE THROUGHOUT THE SCHOOL

Customer service happens at Wal-Mart. You go to the customer service
counter when the DVD player you bought last week breaks down and
you want a new one. In education, our relationship to students and parents should be more of a client relationship than a customer one. In a

client relationship, the first thing the provider establishes is the client's need. Once determined, resources are generated to meet the need. When you are in your doctor's office, you want and expect honesty—even if the news is bad. Your professional service provider needs to be caring, but you also want to know what you are up against.

Unfortunately, in education, we often act like Wal-Mart when we are really doing the work of doctors. According to Langford and Cleary (1995), customers are those who receive any of the benefits provided by a system, but in education that notion needs revision. Quality principals and school leaders determine the needs and expectations of their clients and then begin to change the conversation with their constituents by shifting from a customer relationship to a client relationship. Quality schools do more than provide a service; they treat the needs of their clients. They rescue people. They provide a future and hope where there was none before. Designing school systems that serve the needs of the school's clients is the means for providing equity. School leaders will benefit from determining their clients' needs and finding ways to measure whether they are being successful in meeting those needs.

Listening to your public was a recurring theme in the interviews with principals. Actively seeking public input to meet needs requires a different mindset—a switch in emphasis from giving the public information to gathering information from the public about what they need and basing decisions on that information. "The consumers are tired of being told what the schools have done and how great they are" (Bradley 1993, 76). The public wants a chance to say what they think is important, and they need opportunities to do that in meaningful ways so that their concerns can be heard and addressed.

PROVIDE PRIORITY LEADERSHIP: DETERMINE A VISION, BUILD IT, AND COMMUNICATE IT EFFECTIVELY

Goal setting is at the heart of the school-improvement process (Henley 1987), and effective goals cannot be determined without a vision. The role of leadership in any organization, including schools, is to hold everything together, to ensure that all members see the organization as their own and identify with the purpose, mission, and aim of the school (Langford and Cleary 1995). This is done by setting your priorities and sticking to them. Collins (2001) states that one of the first steps to becoming a great company is deciding your core values. Deciding what you will never change is the first milestone on the road to change. Deming's (1986) first and foremost quality-improvement principle is determining a vision that all workers in the system can get behind and support.

Building a vision for the future also implies that school leaders not go from job to job and district to district in an attempt to climb the ladder of corporate success. Servant leaders stay around for the long haul (Fullan 2003) and make lasting improvements over time. Research about schools that have implemented effective, schoolwide behavior-modification programs (Sprague and Golly 2003) suggest that it takes three to five years of sustained effort to change the culture of a school.

Schools didn't get into their present position in a short time, and they can't change in a short time. It takes long-term thinking to provide long-term solutions. If leadership is not willing to make such a commitment, then the organization will simply shift from year to year as the winds of politics bring new leaders. Many of the principals interviewed attributed their success to the fact that they made an investment and commitment to a school to build the capacity of that particular place. Because of the stress of efficiency and the cost of providing equity to achieve excellence, successful businesses have already learned and are applying the management philosophy for the twenty-first century—you can't be all things to all people (Treacy and Wiersema 1996). You must determine what is important and deliver on it.

BUILD LEADERSHIP CAPACITY AND TEAMING

In the high-tension days of shrinking resources, principals who are managing effectively are training and enlisting the help and support of others in creative and unique ways. One of the high school principals interviewed had an elaborate system with over thirty parents coming in to call home for each and every student that was absent on a daily basis. Another one enlisted the religious community to help supervise the campus during lunch, and another principal had an elaborate reading mentor program built with volunteers.

Stephen Covey (1989) discusses the importance of effective leaders helping those they work with move from dependence to independence to interdependence—and it is through interdependence that teachers have the authority to act on their own and have the organization's best interests at heart. They are deeply connected to teams of professionals to accomplish things they cannot do on their own. The restructuring of education toward quality will not happen with administrators alone. Teachers must be involved and must work side by side with administrators to do it. Teams do crucial work in schools: They find solutions to complex problems, and they find ways to improve.

Empowering teachers through leadership development and teaming accomplishes another vital task: it flattens the hierarchy. According to Bradley's (1993) summary of the research on empowerment, when teachers are empowered, they have increased roles in decision making at the building level. They are more engaged in problem solving, and there is more collaboration among teachers and between teachers and administrators. The culture is more professional in nature. Although *empowerment* is a trendy, popular word in organizational circles, it is a vital concept in building a quality organization. Unfortunately, many people talk about empowerment without understanding what it is or having the knowledge or skills to implement it. According to Bowles and Hammond, "empowerment means giving employees the authority and information they need to make wise business decisions and solve problems" (1991, 157).

Success depends upon the interdependency between collaboration and goals (Schmoker 1996). Goals give teamwork meaning. High expectations and strong results for schools are not achieved by teachers working in isolation.

Empowered teachers are motivated to inspect their own work through self-reflection and review their own classroom data to make improvements in their instruction. There is less need for administrators to tell them what they are doing wrong. The result is an increase in efficiency. As long as there are clear standards and effective ways to measure student progress toward those standards, teachers will take more and more ownership of their ability to get students to those standards if they feel empowered.

EMPHASIZE CONTINUOUS IMPROVEMENT IN ALL AREAS BY FOCUSING ON DATA-DRIVEN RESULTS

Central to the concept of quality is the notion of continuous improvement through learning and self-reflection (Bonstingl 2001). Principals committed to their own learning attend classes, conferences, and workshops. They also are engaged in reading and writing about their profession. According to those interviewed, the principal should be a strong advocate for instruction and stay current with research and best practice. Standards provide a framework of accountability for teachers. Successful principals visit the classroom often to provide coaching and help teachers weave best practices into the standards.

Committed, effective school leaders know there is almost no job performance that cannot be improved upon, and quality teachers seek to constantly improve (Sullo 1997). It is clear from the interviews that none of these principals is satisfied with the status quo. Even those who achieved an "exemplary" report card rating don't mention that rating in discussions about quality. Quality in the eyes and minds of principals is much more than a report card rating—even though they use that rating as a political tool within their communities. Quality is tied to continuous improvement in what matters—providing a launching pad for a successful life beyond school by lighting the fuse of learning through meeting the educational needs of their students.

Successful organizations understand that the key to quality can be summed up in one word—results, both short- and long-term (Schmoker 1996). Principals and school leaders who focus a laserlike vision on results develop a results-orientated culture that is data driven. Data gathered from all possible avenues can be used to measure progress, celebrate successes, and pinpoint areas of improvement. Test data should include not only performance level but also performance gains over the test administration period. Performance gains can be thought of as "value added" to the school even though the performance level might still be average (Coleman 1995).

Continuous progress schools collect and analyze qualitative as well as quantitative data to make high-quality decisions. Quantitative data will help principals improve their quality of product, and paying attention to qualitative data gathered through surveys, interviews, and observations will help them improve the quality of experience students have in school. Quality of product and quality of experience are not mutually exclusive. One principal reported that the successful football season they experienced had a ripple effect throughout the school and provided a "can do" attitude that resulted in higher attendance rates and increased student learning. When quality of experience is at high levels, students want to be at school, and the quality of product increases.

When educational reformer Lorraine Monroe transformed a low-performing school in central Harlem into a place of high expectations and greatly improved academic achievement, she did it by paying attention to quality of both product and experience:

> I tell students that the purpose of a school is to help them see that where they are now is not where they're always going to be. So, while we're going to do the reading and math, we're also going to pay soccer and volleyball; learn to fence; learn to love art, music, dance and drama; and visit museums and go on other field trips. (Checkley 2004, 71)

Effective school leaders are able to use data to move their organizations toward output-driven systems. Output-driven schools look to their students, parents, and community (including higher educational systems) for measures of success. This is very different from an administrative-driven school system, which looks to the superintendent for approval. School leaders can produce output-driven schools through a combination of *academic press*, ongoing support, and maximizing positive, facilitative relationships between teachers and students (Coleman et. al. 1997; Hoy, Sweetland, and Smith 2002).

In 1977 Aspy and Roebuck published a book called *Kids Don't Learn from People They Don't Like*. Their book was built on a hypothesis of Carl Rogers (1957), who in the 1950s posited that students would learn more and behave better if they were taught by high-facilitative teachers (individuals with high levels of understanding, caring, genuineness, and friendliness). Aspy and Roebuck tested Rogers's idea with more than 10,000 students in classrooms all over the country and came to the conclusion by which they titled their book (McEwan 2002).

The term *academic press* was developed during the 1970s. Although it originally applied to the pressure students, parents, and communities place on schools to achieve established goals and values, over the years it has come to mean the normative emphasis schools and teachers place on academic excellence (Shouse 1997). Researchers (Murphy et al. 1982) have cited academic press as a necessary by-product of effective schools and claim it is a natural result of increasing expectations, accountability, and taking responsibility for student learning outcomes.

To maximize the use of data, two of the principals interviewed have schoolwide teams that serve as a quality control circles through ongoing data analysis to a much greater degree than a site council does. These teacher teams have half-day and full-day workshops throughout the school year at which they collectively analyze and review school profile data with district office representatives and as a result make detailed plans for improving practice and performance in the classroom and school.

MOVE AWAY FROM "BOSS MANAGEMENT" TO "LEAD MANAGEMENT"

Management plays the most crucial role in whether a school will achieve quality. Glasser (1992) states that there are two types of leadership: boss management and lead management. *Boss management* contains four basic elements. First, the boss sets the tasks and standards for the workers and does so without consulting the workers. Second, the boss tells rather than shows the workers how to do the work and rarely asks for input. Third, the boss (or someone the boss designates) inspects or grades the work, and finally, when workers resist, the boss uses coercion to achieve the set goal.

Lead management, on the other hand, is completely different. The leader engages the workers in a discussion of the quality of the work to be done and solicits their input. The leader (or designee) shows or models how the job is to be done. The workers are asked if they have a better way. Then the leader asks the workers to inspect and evaluate their own work. Finally, the leader facilitates and shows the workers he or she has done everything possible to provide the workers with the best tools and workplace possible, and creates a noncoercive atmosphere (Glasser 1992).

The lead manager's job is to communicate a compelling vision of quality and inspire cooperation (Crawford, Bodine, and Hoglund

1993). The literature has many examples of effective leadership for the twenty-first century. Conley and Goldman (1994), *Leading Without Power* (De Pree 1997), and *Servant Leadership* (Greenleaf 2002) all discuss the characteristics of lead management. The lead manager devotes his or her time and energy to running the system so workers can focus on doing quality work.

The focus of boss management is on authority, doing what you are told, and pleasing your supervisor. The focus of lead management is producing a quality product that will meet the needs of the customer. Lead management is based on commitment to the well-articulated purpose. Those under boss management are just trying to get done so they can go home.

Lasting change and effective restructuring in schools come from commitment, not authority, and the leader is the primary agent for the improvement of the system. The aim of leadership should be to help people do a better job. Lead managers do not judge their workers and rank individual performances. Instead, they judge their own performance as they observe workers and determine what they need to do to see improvement. In this way, the lead managers build trust and encourage everyone to improve. They also provide an environment in which everyone can experience pride in their work and help each other to perform to their greatest potential—all in a manner consistent with the school's purpose (Crawford, Bodine, and Hoglund 1993).

Most of the principals interviewed for this study can be characterized as lead managers, and that is why they are experiencing success in balancing the values of excellence, efficiency, and equity. When asked what recommendations he had for other principals, one school leader at a medium-sized rural high school responded in the spirit of a lead manager by saying, "you need to build in your staff a sense of confidence that you work with them, they don't work for you—that we are all in this together."

WORK WITH THE CENTRAL OFFICE

Principals must work in cooperation with their central office if they want to have a quality school. It is easy to fall into the trap of blaming the district office or seeing "downtown" as more needless bureaucracy, and that tone could be heard in some of the interviews, but research done by the Center for Effective Schools (Lezotte 1990) shows that when schools bypass the central office, their reform efforts are far less successful than schools that are aligned with the district office and receive their support and encouragement. Active involvement by the superintendent is a powerful indicator of a school's effectiveness in improvement. School board and community involvement is also important, but not as crucial as central office support. The principals interviewed showed a strong connection to the central office, especially when it came to gaining support for reform.

BUILD A SENSE OF COMMUNITY AND CREATE SMALLNESS

Creating a school community is an important component in achieving an high quality of experience. Based on a study of 357 secondary schools, Bryk and Driscoll (1988) describe three concepts found in schools that exhibit a community. The first is a core set of beliefs about what students should learn, how people in the school should behave, and the kind of adults students could become (end product). Second, in schools with high levels of community, the teachers and staff members develop activities capable of linking all school members to one another and the school's mission. Third, social relations throughout the school are infused with an attitude of caring and collegiality. If all these components—common beliefs, schoolwide activities, and a caring atmosphere—are present, the school can be characterized as a community (Lehman 1993).

Principals can greatly increase the quality of experience students have in their schools by building a sense of community. This can be done through activities, events, and projects that link the whole school together. It can also be achieved by developing a core set of beliefs and values that everyone in the school works toward and by the staff exhibiting a caring attitude in all interactions.

The sheer size of many of our large high schools and middle schools works against what the research says is important for creating effective schools that have high levels of both quality product and experience

(Gregory and Sweeney 1993; Sizer 1984; Gregory and Smith 1987; Howley and Harmon 2000). In small schools, it is easier to identify the needs of students. There might not be as many resources available to meet those needs, but it is easier to determine the needs because the quality of relationships is higher.

Principals of large schools need to find ways to create smallness within their environment so that relationships can be maximized. Many of the principals interviewed stressed the importance of relationships to school success and achieving excellence, including learning the names of every student in the school. That is difficult to do when there are more than 500 students. With small schools, it is much easier to build relationships and create community. The development of small learning communities within a large school is another way this can be accomplished. Successful high school academies in Oakland were able to demonstrate that the vicious cycle of inner-city poverty and poor academic performance can be broken through small learning communities (Guthrie and Guthrie 1993). The Federal Small Schools Initiative and the Bill and Melinda Gates Foundation are currently strong supporters of breaking large schools into smaller ones, and they are backing their reform innovations with large grant opportunities for those that qualify and are willing to make the transition to small schools.

However, one principal mentioned that in a budget shortfall, there are resources in terms of qualified teachers, course offerings, and opportunities in a large school and school district that small schools and districts do not have. Another principal mentioned that small schools will have a very difficult time meeting the demands of the No Child Left Behind Act, so in the light of efficiency, there is a balance in school size that principals must understand and manage effectively.

BUILD AND USE NETWORKS

The most frequent advice principals had for other school leaders was the importance of meeting with other principals to share ideas and resources and to commiserate with one another. They advocated time without agendas in which principals could learn from their peers how to solve complex problems. Reformer Roland Barth (1996) has advocated and helped to develop programs for principals to create these kinds of networks. Many principals feel the collective wisdom between leaders is an untapped resource that needs to be utilized. Establishing partnerships with other schools and districts for the purpose of building networks of support is a definite need and desire for principals. Such partnerships can help principals keep their focus on what matters to them the most, which, in the words of one of the respondents from a large suburban middle school, is "Do the right thing for kids and do not let others pressure you into making decisions that are not in the best interest of the children."

USE TENSION GENERATED FROM EXTERNAL DEMANDS AS IMPETUS FOR GROWTH

New policy creates change, and change generates tension for schools and the people who manage them. This tension, though often stressful, can be used for improvement in the areas of excellence, equity, and efficiency in our public schools. As principals embrace the tension and view it as a positive driver of change, they can help their staff adjust to change more effectively and quickly. The result will be greater school improvement and effective reform.

Using tension in a positive way requires orientating staff members toward something that is positive so that they do not get discouraged when the going gets tough. If principals develop their own definitions about what quality means and communicate that vision to their staff, it will help them stay on track when efficiency pressures weigh heavy. Following are some of the definitions of quality I was given in my interviews:

> Every child being actively and meaningfully engaged in the outcomes, and I would tie in with that community. I have strong beliefs in parent support, community support. I believe also that quality education is reflected in what my community thinks about us. If you go around and ask what people think about our school, you are going to get a favorable response.— *large suburban high school*

> One where kids feel good about themselves and good about the progress they make. Teachers, parents, kids, all have a degree of pride in the learn-

ing community at school. They feel good about being there and about coming.—*medium-sized rural high school*

The quality school model, in my opinion, has a lot of validity. It meets every student's needs almost when they walk into the building. Under NCLB—which I think has some great tenets to it—we almost have an IEP for every kid. No child is left behind. That we have after-school tutorials, that we have remediation, that we allow students to take the test over again. All of those are measures of quality.—*small rural high school*

Quality is a complete package. More than test scores. A quality school is where people want to be.—*medium-sized rural K–8 school*

Kids are on task, and they find meaning in their learning. Teachers are working together toward high standards and people know each other and there is good communication in and among groups, including parents. There is support from the leadership and there is an articulated vision by the school leaders. There is a feeling of working together.—*large suburban high school*

INSTILL HOPE AND MAKE IT FUN

To flourish, school leaders must nurture choice and client satisfaction within their programs. Client satisfaction in education today consists of achieving excellence through equity and using the lever of efficiency to make the most of limited resources. Effective principals know how to instill hope in the midst of difficult and trying situations. "Leaders with hope are less likely to panic when faced with immediate and pressing problems. . . . Articulating and discussing hope when the going gets rough re-energizes teachers, reduces stress, and can point to new directions" (Fullan 1998, 11). Hope must be pursued not because success is guaranteed but because the cause of public education is worth fighting for.

I was amazed again and again during the interview sessions as principals talked about opportunity and hope in the midst of difficult times for public education. Principals are remarkable, possibility-oriented people who—even with shrinking resources—do not consider shortchanging children an option. Public education needs people who can provide the kind of hope this principal expressed:

> We are absolutely determined that they can gut us as far as they want and we are not going to let the children feel it too much. And there is no question that our class sizes have increased because of the continued cutbacks, and if you look into today's paper, the shortfall is gigantic compared to what they were expecting so the cuts will be even deeper, but we remain committed, nonetheless, to delivering good education.—*large suburban middle school*

The final element crucial for an improvement effort to be effective and sustainable over time is that of enjoyment. In approaching the difficult work of change, Flower (1993) states that people need creative environments that have elements of play and laughter in order to discover solutions to complex problems.

Teachers need to find joy in their work—especially when they are undergoing the difficult work of change. The intentionality of change requires a great deal of focus and attention. Long-term improvements via the route of overcoming adaptive challenges are not accidents. Sustained focus, effort, and energy are constantly being required to achieve success. Sustained focus is exhausting. The complexity of change is stressful. Teachers will leave environments that are exhausting and stressful, or worse yet, they will tune out if they are exhausted and stressed—just to survive.

Edward Deming (1986), the founding father of today's emphasis on data-driven decision-making pioneered the work of quality and continuous improvement for more than 50 years. However, a study of his principles for success reveal that his primary focus was not on data, but on the necessity of the worker finding joy in the difficult labor of continuous improvement. Deming maintained it is the responsibility of management to create an environment free of fear so that the worker can find joy in his labor. Teachers need fearless environments so that they will fully participate in the intentional and complex work of improvement with joy. I maintain that it is only through such environments that schools will achieve the breakthrough results we all would like to experience.

CONCLUSION

Make no mistake about it: Building principals are the single most significant factor when it comes to school improvement and effective reform. There are no simple fixes for public education. The guidelines presented here are proven principles of improvement that are reflected by principals in the field. Applying even one of them in a systematic way will generate positive change for the better. Implementing several of them will dramatically improve the entire culture of a school.

Discussion Points

1. Of the recommendations provided, which is something you would like to see your school implement? How would you go about doing that?
2. Do you have any other recommendations for principals that would help them manage the demand for excellence, equity, and efficiency?
3. How do you define a quality school?

10

RECOMMENDATIONS FOR
POLICYMAKERS

School improvement is not just the work of schools. It also requires the help and support of those who create the policies that govern schools: school board members, district office personnel, and legislators. The following recommendations are a synthesis of data gained from the interviews and current research. This list is by no means exhaustive, but it does provide some helpful guidelines for individuals who are serious about pursuing the complex and arduous task of restructuring our schools around quality through the creation and support of effective policy.

1. Continue to support the development of broad external standards.
2. Use teacher evaluation systems that reinforce quality instruction.
3. Develop meaningful individual and collective incentives for students and schools that reward innovation and risk taking.
4. Keep informed about the needs and wants of school leaders, teachers, parents, and students.
5. Develop effective statewide assessment tools.
6. Increase the receptivity to change through statewide communication forums.
7. Be committed to the *restructuring* of public education.

CONTINUE TO SUPPORT THE DEVELOPMENT OF EXTERNAL STANDARDS

Research strongly supports the connection between external standards and student achievement (Coleman et. al. 1997). The development of meaningful standards over the last dozen years of education reform is positive. Universally, the principals I spoke to support the development of external standards. Not many will argue that schools shouldn't have standards, and principals support external standards developed by experts at the state level in the basic areas of reading, writing, and math. It is clearly the obligation of members of the community—through the appropriate processes—to determine what young people need to know and be able to do as the result of a K–12 public education. Having ways to assess whether those standards have been reached is important for parents and taxpayers as well (Schlechty 1997). It is also important that standards remain broad and focus on the core subjects of reading, writing, and math. The more detailed standards become—to the point of knowing the state capitals by the fifth grade, etc.—the greater the danger of educators moving toward the memorization of facts, as opposed to teaching students how to think, reason, analyze, and create. It is important for states and districts to have standard review committees whose job is to constantly look toward improving standards by keeping them broad. Broad standards prevent the curriculum from becoming narrow. Specific standards narrow the curriculum to the point that districts end up purchasing the textbook the test companies produce (Kohn 1999).

Textbook-driven instruction is demeaning, boring, and unchallenging for most children. The teachers who are most effective at meeting their students' needs use textbooks as a resource to instruction, not as the foundation of instruction. Some of the best teachers don't use textbooks at all and could much better spend the money cost to purchase meaningful materials that support differentiation and authentic, learning-project-based instruction. Broad standards that focus on core subjects help educators in local districts experiment with a wide range of curriculum options, including the movement away from expensive textbooks to the rapidly growing host of online options.

Even though not all of the principals supported legislation aimed at meeting standards or how progress was or was not reported, they all agreed that the establishment of external, state-developed standards has helped improve and focus instruction in the classroom:

> I think we need state guidelines. I don't have any problems with the state academic standards, but the way to get to them. I think the districts need more leeway in that . . . from the tiny little districts, to the big ones—it is so different, and the routes are going to have to be different. With NCLB and not being able to have misassignments and that sort of stuff, that is going to be tough. That is a noose around our neck that is going to be very difficult.—*medium-sized rural high school*

ADOPT TEACHER EVALUATION SYSTEMS THAT REINFORCE QUALITY INSTRUCTION

Teacher evaluation systems need to be developed and implemented that require less inspection and more responsibility for quality to be placed on teachers (Bradley 1993). In such systems, an administrator becomes more of a resource and less of an inspector. Student testing should be analyzed by classroom teachers and then studied to see what children need to learn rather than used for merit pay or hard-to-understand report cards.

Unfortunately, many reforms—even those designed to improve quality instruction—have unintended consequences when implemented. A major portion of No Child Left Behind was aimed at mandating quality instruction. An example one principal provided brings to mind the reality that quality cannot necessarily be mandated:

> *No Child Left Behind* is big deal and I think where it will impact us the most is the quality teacher piece. In a school this size, it is almost impossible not to have a misassigned teacher. With the reduction in staff, I don't know how you can not have one period here or there that won't have a misassigned teacher. Unless you are getting teachers with three or four endorsements, it is going to be next to impossible not to have misassignments as the staff decreases—that is going to be catastrophic for small schools.—*medium-sized rural high school*

In an environment of increased responsibility and expectations, poor teachers either improve their skills or are unable to function. Teachers are forced to become more knowledgeable about assessment data, including its limitations. If policymakers are able to recommend and support a transition from a traditional view of supervision as a hierarchical construct to a more horizontal construct, it will help improve the quality of instruction in the classroom (Germinario and Cram 1998) because horizontal constructs focus on continuous growth and personal improvement through a coaching model rather than the top-down, fear-based "grading" and "evaluation" of employees, which do not necessarily result in a teacher's best ongoing work. There is great variance across the country when it comes to evaluating teachers. Policymakers can encourage quality by helping districts design effective evaluation systems that support continuous learning and growth.

In Lebanon School District, a team of teachers and administrators collaborated over a period of two years to design a teacher evaluation system built on Charlotte Danielson's *Enhancing Professional Practice* (1996) that emphasizes both growth and accountability (Lebanon Supervision and Evaluation Task Force 2001). The *Professional Growth and Accountability* manual in Lebanon raises the ceiling for teachers by giving good teachers the chance to become great, and provides levels of accountability to support teachers who are struggling so that they can reach their full potential.

For the first time, software is now available through companies like eCOVE.net that support continuous improvement through classroom observations. The eCOVE software provides dozens of teacher and student observation tools that allows evaluators and peer mentors to track and manage a great deal of classroom data, which can then be used by administrators and mentor teachers to improve performance. Included with the data is research to support each observation tool.

Every district evaluates its teachers. This is one of the primary jobs of administrators. School board members and district office educators can use this requirement as an opportunity to design evaluation systems that reflect the current thinking about continuous growth and improvement. A great number of districts are using outdated evaluation systems that seem like exercises in futility. Many of them amount to a waste of time when it comes to improving instruction for students. If your school district hasn't overhauled the teacher evaluation system within the last ten years, it most likely does not reflect current thinking and best practice about standards, continuous progress, brain research, and the power of using data to make decisions. It probably could use some improvement.

DEVELOP MEANINGFUL INDIVIDUAL AND COLLECTIVE INCENTIVES FOR STUDENTS AND SCHOOLS THAT REWARD INNOVATION AND RISK TAKING

Although some of the principals do not support state systems of accountability—and the federal system (No Child Left Behind)—the reality is that the accountability movement has brought external testing to the doorstep of every public school in the United States. Quality-of-product indicators via test scores, attendance, and dropout rates are here to stay. Policymakers can help schools make the transition to standards-based instruction by developing meaningful incentives for schools and districts.

We are painfully aware of the sanctions that come with No Child Left Behind. These sanctions begin with school choice and end with school takeover, but the law neglects positive incentives. According to Schiller (1997), for an incentive system to be effective the individuals being tested must know about the examination, see doing well on it as a goal to strive for, and feel attainment of that goal is important. By the same token, they must also see the examination as legitimate or fair. These are big shoes for mandated state tests to fill. If local schools and districts partner with policymakers in the development of accountability and incentives, these examinations can become more meaningful and important to students and teachers.

Successful schools restructure through innovation. Central to that process is the understanding that improvement is an intrinsic, continuous process rather than some achievable end result that is extrinsically imposed. However, most activities that become intrinsic begin with extrinsic motivation—especially the difficult work of school improvement. The entire strategy of initial start-up grants to spark reform is based on the theory that extrinsic motivation is an effective catalyst for long-term intrinsic change. There are no single formulas for success. Continuous improvement is complex, and local differences have a profound impact on what can and cannot be accomplished.

It is clear from the research that quality schools will not emerge without the development of innovative programs (Crawford, Bodine, and Hoglund 1993). However, many principals have stuck their necks out only to have them be chopped off, not crowned. In one school, a culture of resistance to innovation had developed from their experiences:

> It is the innovators who spend a great deal of time and energy out in front on projects and then have those projects get pulled out from under them. Such experiences generates a feeling of wasted and time and energy. There is a feeling almost of punishment if you are doing well and innovating, because that is how it feels when the rug is pulled out from under you. Once that happens a few times, teachers are less likely to buy in and pursue new innovations, and it takes real leadership to get them past those feelings. We've all read the change book, *Who Moved My Cheese*, and we've discovered there is a lot of frustration that goes with trying to follow the cheese. We've discovered that time and frustration can be saved by following a low profile and not being the first to innovate—many times it's the second mouse who actually gets the cheese.—*large urban high school*

Incentives created for change and experimentation can include being able to waive regulations at times (Wilson and Corcoran 1988). In the current structure, districts receive grants for programs they will do. Often when the money arrives, the new program never makes it off the ground, or the innovation proposed is unsuccessful, or the money is used to supplement some other ongoing program.

If districts and schools could receive funds for programs they internally develop, they would be rewarded for what they have already achieved, not what they promise to do. In this way districts can pursue local support for innovative programs rather than run after federal or state grant dollars for untested programs. The incentive money given in recognition of local efforts can come with the stipulation that it be used to refine and perfect the innovation and expand it to other schools and districts. Such a view of improvement will foster innovations to spread. In the current competitive system of grant funding, districts frequently do not share ideas and innovations with other districts because it limits the chance of landing those big dollars.

KEEP INFORMED ABOUT THE NEEDS AND WANTS OF SCHOOL LEADERS, TEACHERS, PARENTS, AND STUDENTS

"Come visit the schools," was the refrain heard most often when I asked school leaders if they had any recommendations for policymakers. It would be an overstatement to say that the principals feel adequately represented by education policymakers, and in the midst of shrinking budgets, those feelings quickly turn sour.

> Anger. I think there is a lot of anger toward the legislation. There is a lot of frustration. I think there are folks that are going to leave education. There are folks here who are going to leave. There is a sort of defeatist attitude that is much more prevalent than before.—*medium-sized rural high school*

> There is a lot of depression right now. There is still the inner determination that they are going to do their best, but they also have the reality that they are not going to be able to do the best as they have been doing.—*large suburban high school*

There is far too much isolation in school systems around the country. Every principal interviewed echoed the need for connection and networking between principals and policymakers. Education is part of the service sector, and as members of the service sector, school leaders are not charged to produce commodities but to produce meaningful change in the situation of the individuals they serve (Henley 1987).

Henley (1987) goes on to maintain that in service industries, it is not the end result only that counts; it is the quality of the experience along the way. Parents already have one means of judging the quality of experience of their children's schools:

> If our kids come home chattering excitedly about something they figured out in class, if they not only can read but do read (on their own), if they persist in playing with ideas and come to think carefully and deeply about things, chances are they attend an excellent school. (Kohn 1999, 200)

Policymakers serve not only children in schools but also parents, the community, teachers, and school leaders. There is no better way than firsthand visits and interviews to know and understand the quality of experience people are having in schools. Reformer Alfie Kohn states the obvious: "The best way to judge schools is by visiting them and looking for evidence of learning and interest in learning. . . . Thoughtful observation is still the best way to gauge the quality of a school, (1999, 201–2). As policymakers find creative ways to keep close to their various constituents, their decisions will more closely match the needs of their clients. In this way, all those involved in schools can have a successful quality of experience.

DEVELOP EFFECTIVE STATEWIDE ASSESSMENT TOOLS

Policymakers should do whatever they can to limit the impact of high-stakes assessments. Many states have moved, or are in the process of migrating, their annual assessments from paper-and-pencil tests to computerized assessments. This is a stroke of brilliance and worth the money to make the change. Not only can computerized assessments adjust the difficulty of the test based on the answers provided, but they can easily allow for frequent breaks and—most important—teachers can have real-time, immediate information about how a student did on the assessment rather than waiting three to six months, after the student is gone for the summer. The true purpose of assessments is to guide instruction. Computerized assessments make that possible. TESA in the state of Oregon and MAPS through the Northwest Regional Lab are two of many such assessments.

Important decisions regarding students and teachers should always be based on multiple sources of evidence. Even the testing industry does not recommend using their assessments as the sole indicator of success for individuals or schools (Meier 2000). Although it is frustrating for school leaders to have state report cards making changes year after year, it is vital that policymakers include multiple data points when it comes to grading schools. If those report cards can include quality of product and quality of experience indicators, the public will be better informed about the quality of their schools. In making the argument for multiple sources of assessment data, researcher Carolyn Shields states, "Education must promote academic excellence, defined not simply in terms of scores on standardized tests, but by high-quality performance indicators on a wide range of outcomes" (2004, 39).

Districts can also be encouraged through incentives to develop their own standards that can be supported by local schools, families, and communities (Meier 2000). There should also be meaningful incentives for districts that discover effective ways to measure achievement of those standards and disseminate those solutions to others. Cross-pollination is healthy for any system, and as states develop ways to encourage cross-pollination between schools and districts, greater growth and achievement will be realized.

Policymakers can improve state-level assessment systems by making sure the tests given are *criterion*-referenced rather than *norm*-referenced. In a criterion-referenced test, student scores are given as compared to achievement of specific criteria (in this case, standards). In a criterion-referenced test, it is possible for everyone to achieve success. Norm-referenced tests compare the students to other students. When standardized test results come back showing a child is in the 75th percentile, that doesn't mean they got 75 percent of the questions right. It means out of every 100 students who took the test, they scored better than 74 of them and worse than 25. Many parents do not understand this distinction, and though it may be helpful for parents to know where their child ranks as compared to other students, it doesn't communicate what a child actually knows. It is more important for parents and especially educators to know how well the child did compared to objective standards so that instruction can be adjusted.

Policymakers should also encourage states to develop performance-based assessments. The most effective means of understanding what a child has actually learned is through performance-based assessments given by a child's classroom teacher (Kohn 1999). In performance-based assessment, students demonstrate what they know and can do through reading and responding to a passage, writing an essay, giving a speech, teaching a lesson, demonstrating a project, or some other performance of their learning. Even though performance-based assessments are more time consuming than multiple-choice tests and quizzes, good teachers frequently use them to determine a child's learning needs and adjust instruction accordingly.

Policymakers can encourage the use of performance-based assessments at the local level by requiring these kinds of tests at the state level. They are more expensive to administer than standardized tests, and they shouldn't be given statewide at every grade level, but some states have developed performance-based assessments in writing and math problem solving at various benchmarks (e.g., grades 5, 8, and 10).

Regardless of whether one believes standardized testing is good, bad, or indifferent, teachers—for the most part—teach what will be tested because they want to help their students be successful, and they want to be represented well by how their students do on the test. When states implement performance-based assessments, teachers change their practice and commit more of their instructional time to authentic, engaging activities that require higher-level thinking and processing to prepare their students for these assessments. The state of Oregon has been giving performance-based assessments in the areas of writing and math problem solving since the mid-1990s. Even in the midst of dwindling resources, our state has stayed committed to using these kinds of assessments because they provide more information than a standardized test score, and we have seen this strategy not only improve student writing and the understanding of mathematical concepts, but also dramatically improve instruction at the classroom level as teachers have migrated more and more to performance-based assessments in the classroom.

INCREASE RECEPTIVITY TO CHANGE THROUGH STATEWIDE COMMUNICATION FORUMS

When it comes to secondary schools, the current situation is alarming at worst and troubling at best. The mainstream secondary school operates largely as it has for the past forty years in spite of increasing equity legislation, excellence initiatives, and efficiency constraints. In the minds of many (including the principals I interviewed), the system is at a breaking point. Despite of all this, the Carnegie unit is still the coin of the realm, and a high school transcript of nonstandardized graded coursework remains the entry pass to higher education. Students are still grouped homogeneously for teacher-directed instruction, and those young people who choose not to, or cannot, succeed in such an environment flow into an ever-increasing network of alternative education settings (Sagor 1999). This is not news to policymakers, the public-at-large, or those working in schools. Most people involved in education would agree that the need for restructuring the U.S. high school has never been more imperative—so why is there so much resistance to change?

Robert Murray Thomas (2002) has applied Newton's laws of motion and developed an inertia theory to explain why change doesn't happen rapidly in education—especially secondary schools. According to his theory, the amount and source of resistance to change is influenced by various conditions: quality of components, organizational complexity, time period, incentives, expense, and communication accuracy. Each of these conditions can have a significant impact on a proposed reform in terms of inertia—in other words, the bigger the problem, the harder it is to move it, but once it gets started, it can take on a life of its own, sometimes resulting in unintended consequences.

My research shows that communication accuracy is a major resistor to change. There is a great gulf between principals viewing excellence as success relative to potential and policymakers seeing it as a high standard achievable by all. In the same vein, when it comes to discussions of equity, there is a big difference between a principal's goal of equal opportunity and the emphasis of policymakers on equal treatment. Recognizing that these differences exist is a major finding because it is these fundamental differences that create resistance to change.

In my interviews with principals, only one mentioned having conversations with the state department regarding policy. This needs to change. Communication is a two-way road. As school leaders contact the state department and lawmakers to share their struggles, successes, and suggestions for improvement, they will experience more success when it comes to implementing policy and reform. To encourage such conversations, policymakers can design statewide forums with school leaders to facilitate greater communication accuracy between local and state governments. School leaders need to make attending and participating in these "improvement forums" a top priority. Opening up the lines of communication does not mean that school leaders and policymakers will always agree, but it will help bridge the gap of understanding between the two, which will result in more effective policy and less resistance to change.

In addition to increasing communication accuracy, these forums can also be designed to help school leaders view the tension that comes from external policy demands as a necessary and important component of school improvement. Many educators have argued against the use of policy to exert the pressure of reform, but the truth is most schools would not change if they didn't have to because change is hard work and is uncomfortable. However, once they experience change, most people can see the value in it. Change is a necessary element of growth, and improvement will not occur without some degree of change. Properly designed, these forums can help principals learn to embrace the tension that comes from change rather than resist it.

Improved communication will also help principals understand why the nature of policy and reform is constantly changing and how to deal with that change. More than one principal expressed frustration over what seemed like shifting sands of school reform:

So, policymakers need to get input from everybody, and they have done a pretty good job asking for input, and then they need to implement and stick with the implementation. When they keep changing it, the teachers develop the mentality, "we'll wait them out." I have a hard time with that. If you really value it, make your plan, and then work your plan.—*large suburban high school*

I think some of the state's reform efforts to design tests that align with the curriculum are good attempts. The conversations we've had in the state about student assessments have resulted in some changes, but I think also there has been some negative fallout, too, with some poor decisions that were made in the last ten years—that have been perceived as top down and then been changed and then been changed again. It creates a cynicism; "yeah, we've heard that."—*large suburban high school*

The one area we needed to improve on was our attendance. We have been doing better, we started at 83 percent then up to 87 percent, and now we are pushing 90 percent, so we pushed that over the top, and then we get the communication earlier this year that they changed the formula, so in spite of improvement in all categories this year, we are rated on the low side of satisfactory again because there was a political impetus to change the formula. That is the ugly side of school reform, and it is very frustrating to have the standards for excellence constantly shifting.—*large suburban high school*

BE COMMITTED TO THE RESTRUCTURING OF PUBLIC EDUCATION

Control theory states that behavior is internally motivated and seeks to satisfy the basic needs within us (Glasser 1992). For example, most people would say that students stop talking because the teacher asks for silence. However, control theory asserts that students only keep quiet when they believe it is to their benefit to do what the teacher asks; otherwise they keep talking.

Control theory didn't originate with Glasser. Its roots can be traced to the English philosopher Thomas Hobbes (1588–1679), who believed all of humanity's actions are based on self-concern (Hobbes 1998). First and foremost, people do what is in their best interest. It was this belief that led Hobbes to argue for the establishment of a state or civil government. Because people will do what is in their best interest, external controls and policies are necessary to help people make good choices and keep them from harming one another.

Looking at today's policy environment of accountability in light of Hobbes and Glasser is fascinating. Through Hobbes, we understand why policies of accountability exist. Without them, the public is unsure educators would pursue excellence. However, Glasser's control theory makes the argument that quality or excellence cannot be achieved by the application of external policies alone, and the preponderance of research over the last twenty years of reform shows that restructuring—wholesale change that affects the cultural norms of the school and results in quality—does not happen without people intrinsically motivated working above and beyond the call of duty (Kopczynski 2000). Educators cannot pursue Conley's (1999) "10 Commitments to Restructuring" without moving from compliance to commitment.

Educational policies have produced renewal and reform but have not reached restructuring. Restructuring is internal, and only through restructuring will a school arrive at quality. Policies based on coercion and compliance will not result in quality. Quality goes beyond coercion. Coercion is extrinsically based; quality is internal.

In a study of high schools across the United States, Lee and Smith (2001) found a direct correlation between academic achievement (excellence) and schools that were engaged in practices that were consistent with the school restructuring movement. In other words, restructuring schools were more effective: students learned more and were able to demonstrate that learning in a variety of ways. They also discovered that the restructuring schools were more equitable environments: their students' achievement gain was less differentiated by family social class.

The use of parent volunteers, focusing on cooperative learning, teaming teachers across disciplines, offering mixed-ability classes in mathematics and science, providing teachers with common planning time, offering flexible time for classes, or keeping students in the same homeroom over several years are just some of the more common reform practices used by restructuring schools (Lee and Smith 2001). According to Lee and Smith study, not many high schools in the United States are doing some of these things, and even fewer are doing several of them.

No amount of hard work or extra effort on the part of employees can make up for a poor design of the organizational system. And that is precisely the dilemma we face today in public education. "Employees can only work in the system that is created. They cannot change it" (Orsini 2000, 210). Teachers are caught in a system that is designed for the efficiency of the masses, not the needs of the individual.

Perhaps when the system was designed over 100 years ago, there was a need for structured grade levels and corresponding curriculum, but with the technology available to us now—and from what we know about how the brain works and the importance of learning—we no longer have to be slaves to the age-old system. It was never designed to meet the needs of all learners.

There are really just two ways to change what happens in schools: the support model and the demand model. The support model begins with the notion that the primary role of teachers, administrators, parents, and the community is to help students act on their desire to make sense of the world. The school becomes a place that guides and simulates student interest in exploring what is unfamiliar, constructing meaning, and developing a competence for playing with words and ideas. Improvement follows when students are giving stimulating, worthwhile tasks. They are not just expected to take responsibility for their own learning but are actively assisted in doing so (Kohn 1999). In the support model, students and staff over time become more and more intrinsically motivated to learn and continuously improve.

The majority of reform efforts stem from the demand model. The focus is on compliance with outside rules or policies. As seen from the data I collected, these outside efforts can produce positive change in schools—the use of standards, for instance. But based on the research and my study, I maintain that high levels of quality will not occur via the demand model. Restructuring goes beyond the demand model. It focuses on support—how school leaders can support their students and teachers to bring about meaningful changes in the system that result in continuous improvement.

The demand model is much different. In the demand model, people outside of the classroom decide what the people in it are required to do. Telling teachers exactly what to do and then holding them "accountable" for results is not a commitment to excellence. It reflects, rather, a commitment to an outdated, top-down model of control that originated in Fredrick Taylor's "scientific management" method of speeding up factory production. It was Taylor's belief that precise standards had to be determined in advance before any educational activity occurred in order to achieve the maximum efficiency. Although the business world has since moved past Taylor, Alfie Kohn (1999) argues that much of the current educational reform movement is based on his ideas. In Kohn's opinion, test score improvement is not a sufficient definition of excellence in education. The principals I talked with agreed and were quick to note that state policy is not always written in a way that encourages restructuring:

State policies have hurt us a little bit because they are not as realistic as they need to be for a smaller school. In a larger school, you have so much more support and resources. In the small schools, you don't have that. We do it all. That makes it tough. Enrollment is 500. When I had 1700, it was a whole different animal. I think the ideal high school size is anywhere from 700 to 1000. You still know everyone's name. When you get bigger it's harder. You don't have the personal touch, but when you are smaller you don't have the resources and support you need. State reforms make it very difficult to keep the academic excellence when you are small.—*small rural high school*

A restructuring is needed—a redefining of equity that will touch individuals. The new organizational structure must be more than high-stakes achievement tests. Performance-based assessments via completed projects are still the most accurate way for students to demonstrate what they have learned. It is not seat-time that is important, but a mastery of standards.

It was clear even thirty years ago (Sagor 1999) that meeting the needs of all students would require alterations in the structure and function of the mainstream school. However, changing what many people considered a successful system never received much serious consideration. As a result, public educators saw a rise in alternatives for those who were not successful in mainstream schools. The passage of time, however, has eroded most people's notion that public schools are doing an adequate job.

In a survey conducted by the U.S. Census Bureau in which over 3,000 businesses participated, it was found that the business community feels there is an extraordinary gap between schools and the workplace, and that the object of closer cooperation between the two is not being met. Employers tend to disregard recent graduates' grades and school evaluations. They use consultants for internal training rather than educational institutions. Businesses are getting away from hiring graduates right out of school for career track positions (Caster 1995). In light of news of this kind, escalating school budgets, minor gains in test scores, and students leaving high school still not ready to work, educators and the public alike are ready for restructuring.

CONCLUSION

There is no clearly marked road to restructuring. The journey is arduous and unique. It hinges on the needs, culture, geographic location, community resources, staff, and student body composition of each individual school. However, there are signposts along the way, guiding markers that—if rigorously supported by policymakers—will have a greater result in restructuring school systems to be able to survive the triangle of tension and continuously move toward quality. I have organized these guidelines according the framework of equity, excellence, and efficiency.

Equity: Meeting Student Needs

1. Redefine equity from treating all students the same to providing what every student needs—especially opportunities.
2. Research and develop practical, valid, and reliable ways to measure and determine the intelligence, learning style, and needs of students.
3. Move away from the seat-time Carnegie unit that continually forces the organizational system toward grades, finite curriculum, and teacher-directed instruction and move toward performance-based assessment systems hinged on standards and individual learning needs and styles. Recognizing that students learn in many ways and at different rates, instruction needs to be learning-centered and performance-based.

Excellence: Achievement (Learning) Relative to Potential

1. Provide multiple opportunities for students to take achievement tests and provide small group instruction in the academic areas determined by these achievement tests. Ensure that achievement testing is not the only method used to measure student and school performance. Develop ways to measure both quality of product and quality of experience as demonstrations of excellence.
2. Adopt an orientation toward results, especially those related to student performance. Such an orientation has a direct result on the quality of product.
3. Strengthen the connection between school and community through service learning that provides active academic learning for students and focuses on key transitions between school and work. Providing field experiences along with art, music, technology, and physical education makes classroom learning more meaningful and engaging to students and increases their quality of experience.

Efficiency: Maximizing the Use of Time, Money, Staff, and Resources to Meet Student Needs

1. Encourage school and district leaders to be responsible for restructuring and not to use a lack of resources as an excuse. There must be organizational learning to find hidden efficiencies, and a school's approach to continuous improvement must be embedded in the school's operation (Karathanos 1999). Excuses about funding, blaming others, and waiting for the state department are unacceptable responses. Effective leaders study and apply the quality principle of management by fact, which means basing decisions on measurement, information, data, and analysis. Applying this principle will keep organizations continually moving toward improving how resources are used.

2. Research ways to use technology to deliver, assess, and provide instruction. We have yet to access the vast potential of technology as an educational resource.

3. Reward efficient districts with incentives via recognition and state-level support. Many innovations regarding efficiency can be easily applied in other districts and schools. If schools are encouraged to share efficiency discoveries, everyone will benefit.

Discussion Points

1. What do you think is the single most important action policymakers can take to improve schools? Why?
2. How does the triangle of tension hinder school improvement?
3. How does the triangle of tension generate school improvement?
4. Discuss the value of determining priorities when it comes to surviving the triangle of tension.

GLOSSARY OF TERMS

Breakthrough results: Extraordinary, measurable results. Breakthrough results do not occur by accident. They are achieved through intention by committed leadership over time. Breakthrough results in a school are 90 percent of all students achieving the defined standards as demonstrated by performance assessments and standardized tests.

Critical incidents: A systematic way of analyzing actual events that occur and a subject's response to those events as related to the purpose of a study (Flanagan 1954). In this book, the term is not used to identify specific moments in time or one-time events; rather, it is used to record important issues, concerns, and decisions that principals had to manage or respond to according to the framework of excellence, equity, and efficiency. The recording and analysis of critical incidents was invaluable in helping me form an understanding of how principals manage the demands of excellence, equity, and efficiency.

Efficiency: Resources—what you have and how you use time, money, materials, and services (internal and external services provided by outside sources, e.g., district office, service districts, and the state department of education).

Equity: As used in this book, equal opportunity. The most absolute way to provide equity for students is by meeting their individual needs.

Excellence: As used in this book, success relative to one's potential.

Quality of experience: Data gathered through interviews, surveys, or observations. I have termed this kind of information "soft data" because it is more difficult to measure and more difficult to compare across schools. It takes a greater time investment. When principals talk about the clubs in their school, surveying students to find out their interests, sports programs, parent and community attitudes, providing intramurals, having a great school climate, enrichment opportunities, community service, or mentor programs, these are all examples of quality of experience.

Quality of product: Anything that can be easily measured and compared across schools. Examples are test score achievement, test score improvement, attendance rates, dropout percentage, the number of students going on to education beyond high school, the percent of students achieving a diploma, volunteer hours in the school, the number of teachers with master's degrees or years of teaching experience, and the number of suspensions and expulsions.

Quality School Improvement (QSI) framework: A framework for managing the triangle of tension that puts meeting student needs at the heart of school improvement.

Priority leadership: A philosophy that places an emphasis on leadership over management. Priority leaders work from big ideas—priorities—rather than strategic plans. A certain level of chaos is allowed and embraced so that new ideas and solutions can be found to solve the complex problems generated by the need for excellence, equity, and efficiency.

Professional Growth and Accountability System: An evaluation tool, published in 2001, that promotes growth and provides accountability. It not only defines quality teaching but provides hundreds of examples so that teachers, administrators, and parents know what quality teaching looks, sounds, and feels like.

Signature schools: One of the priorities of Lebanon Community Schools (LCSD). Signature schools have the authority to act and latitude to innovate based upon the vision and values of their school—provided they stay true to the district priority of high achievment.

Student achievement system: A systemic look at student achievement that include the following principles:

- Social promotion and retention are rejected.
- Achievement is the constant and time is the variable. Students progress through learning benchmarks as they demonstrate proficiency.
- Authentic learning of the intended curriculum is the desired outcome.

Tension generator: Anything that creates pressure for change. The term is used in this book to describe policies that are based on one or more of the following values: excellence, equity, and efficiency.

Triangle of tension: A visual representation of the tension that exists among excellence, equity, and efficiency.

REFERENCES

Aspy, D. N., and F. N. Roebuck. 1977. *Kids don't learn from people they don't like*. Amherst, MA: Human Resource Development Press.

Barth, R. 1996. *The principal learner: A work in progress*. Cambridge, MA: Geraldine R. Dodge Foundation.

———. 2001. *Learning by heart*. San Francisco: Jossey-Bass.

Berne, R., and L. Stiefel. 1984. *The measurement of equity in school finance: Conceptual, methodological and empirical dimensions*. London: John Hopkins University Press.

Bonstingl, J. J. 2001. *Schools of quality*. 3rd ed. Thousand Oaks, CA: Corwin Press.

Bowles, J., and J. Hammond. 1991. *Beyond quality: How 50 winning companies use continuous improvement*. New York: Putnam.

Boyd, W. L., and C. T. Kerchner. 1988. *The politics of excellence and choice in education*. New York: Falmer Press.

Bracey, G. W. 1994. *Transforming America's schools: An Rx for getting past blame*. Arlington, VA: AASA Publications.

———. 2003. *The end of childhood and the destruction of public schools*. Portsmouth, NH: Heinemann.

Bradley, L. H. 1993. *Total quality management for schools*. Lancaster, PA: Technomic Publishing Company.

Brown-Hedrick, K. 2002–2003. Comprehensive school reform: How can schools afford it? *National Forum of Educational Administration and Supervision Journal* 19(3):20–30.

Bryk, A., and M. Driscoll. 1988. *The high school as community: Contextual influences, and consequences for students and teachers.* Madison, WI: National Center on Effective Secondary Schools.

Caldwell, B. J., and J. M. Spinks. 1998. *Beyond the self-managing school.* Philadelphia: Falmer Press.

Carlson, R. V. 1996. *Reframing & reform: Perspective on organization, leadership, and school change.* White Plains, NY: Longman Publishers.

Caster, D. 1995. Letter from the editor. *QED News* 2(2):2.

Chase, B. (2000). Making a difference. In *Will standards save public education?* ed. J. Cohen and J. Rogers. Boston: Beacon Press.

Checkley, K. 2004. A is for audacity: Lessons in leadership from Lorraine Monroe. *Educational Leadership* 61(7):70–72.

Clegg, A. J. 2000. Market-driven education. In *Restructuring education: Innovations and evaluations of alternative systems,* ed. S. Hakim, D. J. Ryan, and J. C. Stull, 183–95. Westport, CT: Praeger.

Clinchy, E. 1992. Public schools of choice: School reform in the desegregating urban districts of Massachusetts. In *Restructuring the schools: Problems and prospects,* ed. J. J. Lane and E. G. Epps, 165–85. Berkeley, CA: McCutchan Publishing.

Cohen, D. K., and P. Neufeld. 1981. The failure of high schools and the progress of education. *Daedalus* 110: 69–90.

Coleman, J. S. 1995. Achievement-oriented school design. In *Restructuring schools: Promising practices and policies,* ed. Maureen T. Hallinan, 11–28. New York: Plenum Press.

Coleman, J. S., et al. 1966. *Equality of educational opportunity.* Washington, DC: U.S. Government Printing Office.

———. (1997). *Redesigning American education.* Boulder, CO: Westview Press.

Collins, J. 2001. *From good to great: Why some companies make the leap—and others don't.* New York: Harper Press.

Conley, D. T. 1999. *Roadmap to restructuring: Charting the course of change in American education.* 2nd ed.. University of Oregon: ERIC Clearinghouse on Educational Management.

Conley, D. T., and P. Goldman. 1994. *Facilitative leadership: How principals lead without dominating.* Eugene, OR: Oregon School Study Council

Cookson, P. W. 1994. *School choice: The struggle for the soul of American education.* New Haven, CT: Yale University Press.

Coombs, P. H., and J. Hallak. 1972. *Managing educational costs.* New York: Oxford University Press.

Cooper, L. 2004, February. *Using data to ask the right questions: Addressing the achievement gap with data.* Presented at a meeting of the American Association of School Administrators. San Francisco, CA.

Covey, S. R. 1989. *The seven habits of highly effective people: Powerful lessons in personal change.* New York: Simon & Schuster/Fireside Books.

Cramer, S. R. 1996. Assumptions central to the quality movement in education. *Clearing House* 69(6): 360–65.

Crawford, D. K., R. J. Bodine, and R. G. Hoglund. 1993. *The school for quality learning: Managing the school and classroom the Deming way.* Champaign, IL: Research Press.

Cunningham, L. L. (1972). Accountability: Watchword for the '70s. In *Accountability in American education,* ed. F. J. Sciara and R. K. Jantz. Boston: Allyn & Bacon.

Danielson, C. 1996. *Enhancing professional practice: A framework for teaching.* Virgina: ASCD.

Darling-Hammond, L. 1997. *The right to learn: A blueprint for creating schools that work.* San Francisco: Jossey-Bass.

De Pree, M. 1997. *Leading without power: Finding hope in serving community.* Holland, MI: Shepherd Foundation.

Deming, W. E. 1986. *Out of the crisis.* Cambridge: Massachusetts Institute of Technology.

Dickson, K. 2002, September. *Understanding the federal re-authorization of Title Services.* Presented at the Title I conference by the Oregon Department of Education, Salem, OR.

Edmonds, R. 1979. Some schools work and more can. *Social Policy* 9: 28–32.

Edwards, C. H., and A. E. Wallace. 1993. More on *A Nation at Risk*: Have the recommendations been implemented? *Clearing House* 67(2):85–88.

Elmore, R. F., and D. Burney. 1999. Teaching as the learning profession. In *Handbook of Policy and Practice,* ed. L. Darling-Hammond and G. Sykes, 266–71.

Evans, R. 1995, April 12. Getting real about leadership. *Education Week.*

Firestone, W. A., M. E. Goertz, and G. Natriello. 1997. *From Cashbox to Classroom: The struggle for fiscal reform and educational change in New Jersey.* New York: Teachers College Press.

Flanagan, J. C. 1954. The critical incident technique. *Psychological Bulletin* 51(4):327–58.

Ford, D. Y., and D. A. Harmon. 2001. Equity and excellence: Providing access to gifted education for culturally diverse students. *Journal of Secondary Gifted Education* 12(3):141–48.

Fowler, F. C. 2000. *Policy studies for educational leaders: An introduction.* Upper Saddle River, NJ: Prentice-Hall.

Friedman, M. 1962. *Capitalism and freedom.* Chicago: University of Chicago Press.

Fuhrman, S. H. 1999. *The new accountability.* Washington, DC: U.S. Department of Education.

Fullan, M. 1998. Leadership for the 21st century: Breaking the bonds of dependency. *Educational Leadership* 55(7):6–11.

———. 2003. *The moral imperative of school leadership.* Thousand Oaks, CA: Corwin.

———. 2004, February. Leading in a culture of change. Presented at the meeting of the American Association of School Administrators, San Francisco, CA.

Gardner, H. (1983). *Frames of mind: The theory of multiple intelligences.* New York: Basic Books.

Gardner, J. 1961. *Excellence: Can we be equal and excellent too?* New York: Harper.

Gardner, W. E. 1984. A nation at risk: Some critical comments. *Journal of Teacher Education* 35(1):13–15.

Germinario, V., and H. Cram. 1998. *Change for public education: Practical approaches for the 21st century.* Lancaster, PA: Technomic Publishing.

Gibson, A., and S. Asthana. 1998. School performance, school effectiveness and the 1997 white paper, excellence in education. *Oxford Review of Education* 24(2):195–211.

Glasser, W. 1992. *The quality school: Managing students without coercion.* New York: Harper & Row.

Greenleaf, R. K. 2002. *Servant leadership: A journey into the nature of legitimate power and greatness.* Mahwah, NJ: Paulist Press.

Gregory, T. B., and G. R. Smith. 1987. *High schools as communities: The small school reconsidered.* Bloomington, IN: Phi Delta Kappan.

Gregory, T. B., and M. E. Sweeney. 1993. Building a community by involving students in the goverance of the school. In *Public schools that work: Creating community,* ed. G. A. Smith, 101–28. New York: Routledge.

Gross, M. U. M. 1989. The pursuit of excellence or the search for intimacy? The forced-choice dilemma of gifted youth. *Roeper Review* 11(4):189–94.

Guthrie, L. F., and G. P. Guthrie. 1993. Linking classrooms and communities: The health and media academies in Oakland. In *Public schools that work: Creating community,* ed. G. A. Smith, 155–77. New York: Routledge.

Hanushek, E. A., et al. 1994. *Making schools work: Improving performance and controlling costs.* Washington, DC: The Brookings Institution.

Heifetz, R. 2004, February. Adaptive leadership. Presented at the meeting of the American Association of School Administrators, San Francisco, CA.

Heimann, B. A., and J. Sikula. 2001–2002. How can organizational development principles be used to improve schooling? *National Forum of Educational Administration and Supervision Journal* 19(1):5–9.

Helbowitsh, P. S. 1990. Playing power politics: How "A Nation at Risk" achieved its national stature. *Journal of Research Development in Education* 23(2):82–88.

Henley, M. 1987. School improvement policies: A response from the UK perspective. In *Improving the quality of schooling: Lessons from the OECD international school improvement project*, ed. D. Hopkins. New York: Falmer Press.

Hobbes, T. 1998. *On the citizen: Thomas Hobbes.* Ed. R. Tuck and M. Silverthorne. New York: Cambridge University.

Howley, C. B., and H. L. Harmon. 2000. *Small high schools that flourish: Rural context, case studies, and resources.* Washington, DC: U. S. Department of Education.

Hoy, W. K., S. R. Sweetland, and P. A. Smith. 2002. Toward an organizational model of achievement in high schools: The significance of collective efficacy. *Educational Administration Quarterly* 38(1):77–93.

Johns, R., E. L. Morphet, and K. Alexander. 1983. *The economics and financing of education.* 4th ed. Englewood Cliffs, NJ: Prentice-Hall.

Johnson, J. 2004. What school leaders want. *Educational Leadership* 61(7):24–27.

Karathanos, D. 1999. Quality: Is education keeping pace with business? *Journal of Education for Business* 74(4):231–36.

Kelleher, J. 2000. Developing rigorous standards in Massachusetts. In *Coping with standards, tests, and accountability: Voices from the classroom*, ed. A. A. Glatthorn and J. Fontana. Washington, DC: National Education Association.

Kohn, A. 1999. *The schools our children deserve: Moving beyond traditional classrooms and "tougher standards."* Boston: Houghton Mifflin.

Kopczynski, M. 2000. Restructuring schools through school-based management: Experiences and insights from 12 districts. In *Restructuring education: Innovations and evaluations of alternative systems*, ed. Simon Hakim, Daniel. J. Ryan, and Judith. C. Stull. New York: Praeger.

Kozol, J. 1991. *Savage inequalities: Children in America's schools.* New York: Crown Publishing.

Lampman, R. J. 1977. Concepts of equity in the design schemes for income distribution. In *Equity, income, policy: Comparative studies in three worlds of development*, ed. I. L. Horowitz. New York: Praeger.

Langford, D. P., and B. A. Cleary. 1995. *Orchestrating learning with quality.* Milwaukee, WI: Quality Press.

Lankford, H., and J. Wyckoff. 1995. Where has the money gone? An analysis of school district spending in New York. *Educational Evaluation and Policy Analysis* 17: 195–218.

Lashway, L. 1999. Accountability. In *National Association of Elementary School Principals*. Eugene, OR: ERIC Clearinghouse on Educational Management.

Lebanon Supervision and Evaluation Task Force. 2001. *Professional growth and accountability: Program manual and resource guide for 21st century supervision and evaluation for licensed teaching professionals.* Lebanon, OR: Lebanon Community School District.

Lee, V. E., and J. B. Smith. 2001. *Restructuring high schools for equity and excellence: What works.* New York: Teachers College Press.

Lehman, D. 1993. Building community as an alternative secondary school. In *Public schools that work: Creating community,* ed. G. A. Smith, 86–99. New York: Routledge.

Lezotte, L. W. 1990. Lessons learned. In *Case studies in effective schools research,* ed. B. O. Taylor, 195–99. Madison, WI: National Center for Effective Schools.

Lim, L., and J. Tan. 1999. The marketization of education in Singapore: Prospects for inclusive education. *International Journal of Inclusive Education* 3(4).

Lloyd, C. 2000. Excellence for all children false promises! The failure of current policy for inclusive education and implications for schooling in the 21st century. *International Journal of Inclusive Education* 4(2).

Lucas, J. R. 1997. Against equality. In *Equality: Selected readings,* ed. L. P. Pojman and R. Westmoreland, 104–12. New York: Oxford University Press.

Lunenburg, F. C. 1992. The current educational reform movement. *Education & Urban Society* 25(1):3–18.

McEwan, E. 2002. *Ten traits of highly effective teachers: How to hire, coach, and mentor successful teachers.* Thousand Oaks, CA: Corwin.

Meier, D. 2000. Educating a democracy. In *Will standards save public education?* ed. J. Cohen and J. Rogers. Boston: Beacon Press.

Monk, D. H. 1990. *Educational finance: An economic approach.* New York: McGraw-Hill.

Morgan, M. I., A. A. Cohen, and H. Hershkoff. 1995. Establishing educational program inadequacy: The Alabama example. *University of Michigan Journal of Law Reform* 28: 559–98.

Morris, J. E. 1972. Accountability: Watchword for the '70s. In *Accountability in American education,* ed. F. J. Sciara and R. K. Jantz. Boston: Allyn & Bacon.

Mort, P. R., W. C. Reusser, and J. W. Polley. 1960. *Public school finance.* New York: McGraw-Hill.

Moses, M. C. 1990. *The peak performance school.* New York: J. L. Wilkerson Publishing.

Murgatroyd, S., and C. Morgan. 1993. *Total quality management and the school.* Philadelphia: Open University Press.

Murnane, R. J. 2000. The case for standards. In *Will standards save public education?* ed. J. Cohen and J. Rogers. Boston: Beacon Press.

Murphy, J. F., M. Weil, P. Hallinger, and A. Mitman. 1982 Academic press: Translating high expectations into school policies and classroom practices. *Educational Leadership* 40:22–26.

National Commission on Excellence in Education. 1983. *A nation at risk: The imperative for educational reform: A report to the Nation and the Secretary of Education.* Washington, DC: U.S. Department of Education.

National Joint Committee on Learning Disabilities. 1991. School reform: Opportunities for excellence and equity for individuals with learning disabilities. *Journal of Learning Disabilities* 25(5):276–80.

Natriello, G., E. L. McDill, and A. M. Pallas 1990. *Schooling disadvantaged children: Racing against catastrophe.* New York: Teachers College Press.

Odden, A. R., D. Monk, Y. Nakib, and L. O. Picus. 1995. The story of education dollar: No academy awards and no fiscal smoking guns. *Phi Delta Kappan* 77:161–68.

Okun, A. 1975. *Equality and efficiency: The big trade-off.* Washington, DC: Brookings Institution.

Orsini, J. N. 2000. Troubleshooting your activities for excellence. *Total Quality Management* 11(2):207–11.

Patterson, O. 1978. Inequality, freedom and the equal opportunity doctrine. In *Equality and social policy,* ed. W. Feinberg. Chicago: University of Illinois Press.

Porter, A. 1994. National equity and school autonomy. *Educational Policy* 8(4):489–501.

Reeves, D. M. 2000. *Accountability in action: A blueprint for leaning organizations.* Denver: Center for Performance Assessment.

Riley, R. W. 1998. Our teachers should be excellent, and they should look like America. *Education and Urban Society* 31(1):322–29.

Roeper, A. 1996. A personal statement of philosophy of George & Annemarie Roeper. *Roeper Review* 19(1):18–19.

Rogers, C. 1957. The necessary and sufficient condtions of therapeutic personality change. *Journal of Consulting Psychology* 21(1):95–10.

Rosenholtz, S. (1989). *Teachers' workplace: The social organization of schools.* White Plains, NY: Longman.

Rowan, B. 1990. Commitment and control: Alternative strategies for the organizational design of schools. In *Review of research in education,* ed. C. B. Cazden, 353–92. Washington, DC: AREA.

Sagor, R. 1999. Equity and excellence in public schools: The role of the alternative school. *Clearing House* 73(2):72–76.

Schenkat, R. 1993. *Quality connections: Transforming schools through total quality management.* Alexandria, VA: Association for Supervision and Curriculum Development.

Schiller, K. S. 1997 External examinations as an incentive system. In *Redesigning American education,* 119–45. Boulder, CO: Westview Press.

Schlechty, P. C. 1997. *Inventing better schools: An action plan for educational reform.* San Francisco: Jossey-Bass.

Schmoker, M. 1996. *Results: The key to continuous school improvement.* Alexandria, VA: ASCD.

Schmoker, M. J., and R. Wilson. 1993. *Total quality education.* Bloomington, IN: Phi Delta Kappan.

Senge, P. M. 1990. *The fifth discipline.* New York: Doubleday.

Shields, C. M. 2004. Creating a community of difference. *Educational Leadership* 61(7):38–41.

Shouse, R. 1997. Academic press, sense of community, and student achievement. In *Redesigning American education,* 60–79. Boulder, CO: Westview Press.

Silverman, L. 1993. *Counseling the gifted and talented.* Denver: Love Publishing.

Sizer, T. R. 1984. *Horace's comprise: The dilemma of the American high school.* Boston: Houghton Mifflin.

Smith, M. S., S. H. Fuhrman, and J. O'Day. 1994. National curriculum standards: Are they desirable and feasible? In *The governance of curriculum,* ed. S. H. Fuhrman, 12–29. Alexandria, VA: Association for Supervision and Curriculum Development.

Sprague, J., and A. Golly. 2003. BEST training manual: Building positive behavior support in schools. Longmont, CO: Sopris West.

Spring, Joel 1994. *Deculturalization and the struggle for equality: Brief history of the education of dominated cultures in the United States.* New York: McGraw-Hill.

Statistics, National Center for Education. 1995. *The condition of education, 1995.* Washington, DC: U.S. Government Printing Office.

Sternberg, R. J. (1985). *Beyond IQ: A triarchic theory of human intelligence.* Cambridge, MA: Cambridge University Press.

Stevens, M. 1992. School reform and restructuring: Relationship to gifted education. In *Challenges in Gifted Education: Developing Potential and Investing Knowledge for the 21st Century,* 49–55. Columbus, OH: Department of Education.

Stockard, J., and M. Mayberry. 1992. *Effective educational environments.* Newbury Park, CA: Corwin Press.

Stull, J. C., and D. J. Ryan. 2000. Introduction: Current trends in educational restructuring. In *Restructuring education: Innovations and evaluations of al-*

ternative systems, ed. S. Hakim, D. J. Ryan, and J. C. Stull, 1–16. Westport, CT: Praeger.

Sullo, R. 1997. *Inspiring quality in your school: From theory to practice*. Washington, DC: National Education Association.

Tenny, J. 2004. eCOVE: Classroom observation toolkit. Accessed at: www.flowingthought.com.

Thomas, R. M. 2002. *Overcoming inertia in school reform: How to successfully implement change*. Thousand Oaks, CA: Corwin Press.

Tomlinson, C. 1994. The easy lie in educating kids. *Education Digest* 60(2):29–33.

Treacy, M., and F. Wiersema. 1996. *The discipline of market leaders: Choose your customers, narrow your focus, dominate your market*. Reading, MA: Addison-Wesley.

Ulich, R. 1948. *Man and reality : Three dimensions of human experience*. New Haven, CT: The Edward W. Hazen Foundation.

VanTassel-Baska, J. 1997. Excellence as a standard for all education. *Roepler Review* 20(1):9–13.

Verstegen, D. 1994. Reforming American education policy for the 21st century. *Administration Quarterly* 30:365–90.

Wells, A. S., & Crain, R. L. (1992). Do parents choose school quality or school status? A sociological theory of free market education. In P. W. Cookson Jr. (Ed.), *The choice controversy* (pp. 65–82). Newbury Park, CA: Corwin Press.

White, M. W. (1993). Series editor's introduction. In G. A. Smith (Ed.), *Public schools that work: Creating community.* (pp. vii–x). New York: Routledge.

———. (2001). The rhetoric and reality of standards-based school reform. *Educational Policy*, 15(4), 601–610.

Wilson, B. L. & Corcoran, T. B. (1988). *Successful secondary schools: visions of excellence in American public education.* New York: Falmer.

Winch, C. (1996). *Quality and education.* Cambridge, MA: Blackwell Publishers.

Wynne, E. (1972). *The politics of school accountability; public information about public schools.* Berkeley: McCutchan Publishers.

Zimmerman, E. (1997). Excellence and equity issues in art education: Can we be excellent and equal too? *Arts Education Policy Review*, 98(4), 20–27.

INDEX

ABOUT THE AUTHOR

Rob Hess has served children in schools for the past seventeen years as a teacher and principal. He has taught at the middle and high school levels and has administration experience at all levels, K–12. He recently received his doctorate in educational leadership from the University of Oregon in Eugene.

His current assignment is principal at Pioneer School in Lebanon, Oregon, where he lives with his wife, four children, two dogs, several cats, rabbits, and a horse.